LINGUISTIC CHANGE IN PRESENT-DAY ENGLISH

LINGUISTIC CHANGE IN PRESENT-DAY ENGLISH

CHARLES BARBER

UNIVERSITY OF ALABAMA PRESS
UNIVERSITY, ALABAMA

Alabama Linguistic and Philological Series #9

Second Printing, 1966

Published in Great Britain by Oliver and Boyd Ltd
Edinburgh and London 1964

Library of Congress Card Number: 65-24878
Manufactured in the United States of America

Preface

THIS book originated in a series of lectures given in Poland a few years ago to teachers and students of English. Since then, the material has grown constantly, and parts of it have been given as lectures to similar audiences in India, in Pakistan, and also in the United Kingdom, where it has been heard by teachers of English from the U.S.S.R. and by various groups of mixed nationalities. After such lectures, I have frequently been pestered by members of the audience to supply them with the basic material of the lectures in duplicated form; and it is this keen demand that has encouraged me to turn the lectures into a book, despite the obvious shortcomings of the result (it is impossible for a single author to cover such an enormous field without falling into superficiality at many points).

In developing the material into a book, I have tried to adapt it for a rather wider audience, by explaining the technical terms used, and by giving a certain amount of elementary historical background. I hope that this will make it useful for English sixth-formers (or even first-year university students) who are just beginning the historical study of the mother-tongue; and I hope too that this will make it accessible to the layman who is interested in language but who has no specialised knowledge of it. These additions will of course be rather elementary for the overseas teacher, but I hope he will bear with them for the sake of the actual material that the book contains, which illustrates the changes going on in the language to-day.

The aim of the book is to give an account of the changes which have taken place in the English language in England in the past few decades. The idea behind this is that the living language is the right place to begin all language study, and that this applies to historical linguistics as much as to descriptive linguistics. Too often in the past, the student learning the history of the English language has begun with Old English (or even Primitive Germanic, or Indo-European) and plodded on until he got to (at the latest) 1900, when apparently history stopped. To such a student, many of the ideas of historical linguistics will remain abstractions: but if instead he learns these ideas through the language that he hears around him every day, they will have some chance of being meaningful to him.

Some of the material in the book has appeared elsewhere before, in books and articles by various scholars, and the only credit I can claim for this part of the material is that I have brought it together. However, the book is by no means a mere compilation, and there is a good deal of material in it that I have not seen elsewhere; this material I have collected over a period of years while reading books and newspapers, listening to the B.B.C., and just listening to people talking.

My thanks are due to Dr Alvar Ellegård, who read part of the manuscript and offered valuable constructive criticism; to Professor Stephen Ullmann, who suggested to me some useful secondary sources; and to my wife, who prepared the index.

C. L. B.

Leeds
November 1963

Contents

PREFACE   v

I   LINGUISTIC CHANGE   1

II   STANDARD ENGLISH AND DIALECT   16

III   CHANGES IN PRONUNCIATION   33

     LIST OF PHONETIC SYMBOLS   33

       Pure Vowels   33
       Diphthongs   34
       Semi-Vowels   34
       Consonants   34

     1. THE VOWELS   38

       A. GENERAL   38

       B. CHANGES OF VOWEL-QUALITY   41

         (a) *Isolative Changes*   41
         Change in ʌ   41
         Change in ɔː   41
         Change in ai   42
         Centering of short vowels   42

         (b) *Combinative Changes*   42
         Change of ɔː *to* ɔ *before* f, s, *and* θ   43
         Change of juː *to* uː   43
         Diphthongisation of iː *and* uː   44
         Smoothing of diphthongs   45
         Final iː *for* i   46
         Change in final iə   47
         The influence of "dark l*"*   47
         The spread of ə *in unstressed syllables*   48

       C. CHANGES OF VOWEL-LENGTH   49

       D. THE PATTERN OF VOWEL-CHANGE   51

2. THE CONSONANTS   51

    A. GENERAL   51

    B. THE WEAKENING AND LOSS OF CONSONANTS   53
       Final alveolars   53
       Loss of plosives   54
       Simplification of double consonants   54
       Initial ps *and* pt   55
       Initial hw   56
       Loss of h   56

    C. THE DEVOICING OF CONSONANTS   56

    D. THE VOICING OF CONSONANTS   57

    E. INTRUSIVE CONSONANTS   57
       Intrusive stops   57
       Intrusive r   59
       The glottal stop   60

    F. SOME CONSEQUENCES OF THE CONSONANT-CHANGES   61

3. ASSIMILATION   62

4. NEW WEAK FORMS   64

5. DIALECT-MIXING   64

6. CHANGES OF STRESS   65

7. SPELLING PRONUNCIATIONS   66

8. CONTINENTAL PRONUNCIATIONS   72

IV   THE GROWTH OF THE VOCABULARY   77

1. NEW LEARNED FORMATIONS   78

2. AFFIXES   80

    A. PREFIXES   81

    B. SUFFIXES   82

3. COMPOUND WORDS   83

4. BLENDS   89

5. SHORTENING   89

6. CONVERSION   91

7. BACK-FORMATION   94

8. REVIVALS   95

9. PROPER NAMES AND TRADE NAMES   95

Contents

10. INITIALS   97

11. LOAN-WORDS   98

12. INTERNAL LOANS   101

13. SUMMARY   103

     LOSS OF WORDS   104

V   CHANGES IN MEANING   108

VI   GRAMMATICAL CHANGES   129

VII   EPILOGUE   146

     INDEX   151

Chapter I

Linguistic Change

ALL languages are constantly changing; or rather all *living* languages are; and by a *living language* I mean one which is actually being spoken by some human group for the purposes of communication and social co-operation. There are many causes for this process of change: some internal, to do with the nature of the language itself; some external, caused by changes in the culture and society of the speakers, and in the environment in which that culture is set. The rate of change varies from language to language, and from time to time within the same language. Compared with Icelandic, for example, English has changed a great deal in the last thousand years; if a modern Icelander could be taken back in a time-machine, he would probably have little difficulty in understanding his pioneer ancestors of a millennium ago, but a modern Englishman similarly introduced to his ancestors of the tenth century would very quickly (though mistakenly) conclude that their language had nothing to do with his. During this thousand years, however, the pace at which English has changed has varied a good deal: for example, there was much more change between 1350 and 1550 than between 1700 and 1900: between the boyhood of Chaucer and that of Shakespeare lies something of a linguistic gulf, whereas Alexander Pope and Mr T. S. Eliot grew up learning very much the same form of the language.

Some of the ways in which English has changed in the last thousand years can best be suggested by examples, so I have chosen a few short passages of prose from different periods, all dealing with the same subject. The first was published in London in 1785; the theme of the passage is that when a man is wicked he ceases to be a man and becomes an animal.

By degenerating into wickedness, then, they must cease to be men.
. . . What difference is there betwixt a wolf who lives by rapine, and
a robber, whom the desire of another's wealth stimulates to commit
all manner of violence? Is there anything that bears a stronger
resemblance to a wrathful dog who barks at passengers, than a man
whose dangerous tongue attacks all the world? . . . to a deer, than
a coward, who is afraid of his own shadow? to an ass, than a mortal,
who is slow, dull, and indolent? to the birds of the air, than a man
volatile and inconstant? . . . Upon the whole, it is an unquestionable
truth, that a man who forsakes virtue, ceases to be a man; and as it
is impossible that he can ascend in the scale of beings, he must of
necessity degenerate and sink into a beast.

There is very little in that passage which could not have been
written to-day; the constructions and the word-order are completely in accord with present-day usage, and it is only in the
vocabulary that we notice traces of archaism: *betwixt, wrathful,
mortal, forsake*, and *rapine* sound slightly old-fashioned, but there
is only one word, *passenger* in the sense of "passer-by," which
would be quite impossible to-day.

The second passage was written by Queen Elizabeth I in
1593; I have modernised the spelling and punctuation:

So it haps, that whom transformed thou seest with vice, thou mayst
not suppose him a man. The violent robber of others' goods is
fervent in his robberies, swelleth in coveting, and mayst call him
wolf-like; . . . but fearful and flying, feareth and dreadeth that needs
not, and he to deer is compared. The sluggy and dullard languisheth,
and like an ass doth live. The light and unconstant man changes
his intents, and differs so nought from the birds . . . And so it haps,
that he that forsaketh honesty leaves to be a man; for not to be able
to attain a divine state, is turned to the beastly.

Here there are more words that strike us as old-fashioned—
unconstant, haps—and at least one that strikes us as quite unfamiliar: *sluggy*. There are also familiar-looking words used
in unfamiliar senses: *fervent* ("burning with greed"), *fearful*
("afraid, timorous"), *nought* ("not at all"), *leave* ("cease"); here,
changes have taken place in the meanings of the words during
the last three hundred years. In this passage, moreover, there
are differences in morphology and syntax from present-day
English. The form *thou* is used, and the verb that goes with it

has a special ending or inflexion (*seest, mayest*). There are also some third-person singular inflexions in -*eth* (*feareth, dreadeth,* etc.), alongside the normal present-day ending (*needs, changes,* etc.). Constructions are used which would not be possible to-day: for example, the use of *whom . . . him* in the first sentence; the omission of *thou* before *mayst call* in the second sentence; the use of an infinitive after the verb *to leave* ("leaves to be a man"); and the use of *doth live* ("and like an ass doth live") where we should simply write *lives*. In this last example, it should be noted that *doth* is not emphatic: *doth live* is merely a stylistic variant of *liveth*. To-day (if we exclude the emphatic use), we use *do* as an auxiliary only in negative sentences and in questions ("Do you know him?" "I don't know him"), and not normally in declarative sentences ("I know him quite well"): but this regulation of the way *do* is used with verbs is comparatively modern, having become finally established during the seventeenth century. The *do*-forms existed before that, but were used more or less indiscriminately in affirmative, negative, and interrogative sentences, as stylistic variants of the simple verb-forms. Thus in a single scene of *Henry IV, Part I* (III.iii), we find "Do you think I keep thieves in my house?", and "You do not know me, Sir John," but also "A man knows not where to have her." The modern regulation of this kind of *do*-form is probably connected with other changes going on in the language from the late Middle Ages, especially certain typical changes in the word-order of English sentences.

In the Queen Elizabeth passage, then, we see certain clear differences from Present-day English: there are differences of vocabulary, differences of meaning in single words, differences in the endings of verbs (inflexions), and differences in construction. Differences of the same kinds will be seen in the third passage, which was written by Geoffrey Chaucer in the late fourteenth century. I have modernised the punctuation, and made a few changes in spelling.

Than bitidith it, that yif thou seest a wyght that be transformed in to vices, thou ne mayst nat wene that he be a man. For gif he be ardaunt in avarice, and that he be a ravynour by violence of foreine richesse, thou shalt seyn that he is like to a wolf. . . . And yif he be dredeful and fleyinge and dredeth thinges that ne aughten

nat ben dred, man shal holde him lyke to the herte. And yif he be
slowe and astoned and lache, he lyveth as an asse. And yif he be
lyght and unstedfast of corage and chaungeth ay his studies, he is
lickened to briddes . . . than folweth it that he that forletith bountee
and prowesse, he forletith to ben a man. Syn he may nat passe in to
the condicioun of God, he is tourned in to a beest.

Here there are even more unfamiliar words: *ravynour* ("plun-
derer"), *astoned* ("astounded, stunned"), *lache* ("lazy, dull"),
forletith ("abandons"); and words in unfamiliar form: *richesse*
("riches"), *briddes* ("birds"); and words that have since changed
in meaning: *dredeful* ("timorous"), *corage* ("disposition, mind"),
bountee ("goodness"); and of course many words that sound
archaic, though they are perfectly comprehensible. There are
also many more unfamiliar verb-endings: the infinitive often
ends in *-n* (*thou shalt seyn, forletith to ben*); there is a plural ending
in *-en* (*aughten*); there is a past participle *dred*; and a distinction
is made between indicative and subjunctive, as in "thou shalt
seyn that he *is* like to a wolf" (indicative) but "thou ne mayst
nat wene that he *be* a man" (subjunctive). There are also
differences in construction, the most obvious of which is the
use of the double negative *ne . . . nat* ("thinges that *ne* aughten
nat ben dred"). It will be seen that this passage differs more
strikingly from Queen Elizabeth's version (from which it is
separated by only about two hundred years), than hers does
from present-day usage.

My final example is a version of the same passage made by
King Alfred the Great, late in the ninth century. To spare
those readers who have no knowledge of Old English, I will
quote only the first two sentences, but they should be enough to
suggest how much the language changed in the half-millennium
between Alfred and Chaucer.

Forðæm gif ðu swa gewlætne mon metst þæt he bið ahwerfed from
gode to yfle, ne meaht ðu hine na mid ryhte nemnan man ac neat.
Gif ðu on hwilcum men ongitst þæt he bið gitsere ond reafere, ne
scealt ðu hine na hatan mon, ac wulf.

A very large part of the vocabulary of this seems strange to the
modern reader, even when he has mastered the orthography:
gewlætne ("debased"), *ahwerfed* ("turned"), *ongitst* ("perceivest"),

gitsere ("miser"), *reafere* ("robber"), etc. Not a single word in these two sentences, it will be noticed, is of Romance origin: where Chaucer has *transformed*, Alfred has *ahwerfed*; *ardaunt in avarice* becomes *gitsere*; *ravynour by violence* becomes *reafere*; where the later passages have *beast*, Alfred has *neat*. This difference is typical: English is basically a Germanic language, and the vocabulary of Old English is predominantly Germanic in origin, but since the Norman Conquest we have been great importers of words, especially French and Latin words, and to-day there are probably as many words of ultimately Latin derivation in English as there are in French, despite the fact that French is descended from Latin, and English is not. At the same time, of course, we have lost many older words, which is why so much of the vocabulary of Old English seems strange to us.

Another way in which these two sentences differ strikingly from Present-day English is in their word-order. Translated literally word for word, they run: "Therefore if you so debased man meet that he is turned from good to evil, ne can you him not with right name man but beast. If you concerning such man perceive that he is miser and brigand, ne shall you him not call man, but wolf." In some ways this reminds us of modern German, for example in the way the verb *meet* is put at the end of the subordinate clause, and in the way the subject and verb are inverted in the main clause ("ne can you him not"). There are other ways, too, in which Old English reminds us of German: it is a highly inflected language: nouns have grammatical gender (masculine, feminine and neuter), and are declined in four cases in the singular and plural; adjectives are also declined, with both a strong and a weak declension, and have to agree with their nouns; verbs have a variety of inflexions according to number, person, and tense, and have subjunctive as well as indicative forms. In this brief passage, for example, *gewlætne* has an ending to agree with *mon*, accusative singular masculine; *metst* has the ending of the second person singular present indicative; *gode* and *yfle* (nominatives *god* and *yfel*) are in the dative case, governed by the preposition *from*; *hine* is the accusative of the personal pronoun *he* (our modern *him* is derived from the OE dative); *ryhte* is the dative singular of the neuter noun *ryht*; in the phrase *on hwilcum men*, *hwilcum* is the dative singular masculine of the adjective *hwilc*, agreeing with *men*, which is the dative singular of *man* or *mon*; and so on.

Other differences from later usage (for example in the use or omission of the indefinite article) can easily be seen in these two sentences, but enough has been said to suggest the enormous changes that took place between the age of Alfred and that of Chaucer.

In these four passages, then, we see four kinds of ways in which the language has changed. The *vocabulary* has altered: large numbers of new words have appeared in the language, some borrowed from other languages, others coined or constructed; while other words have disappeared altogether.

Secondly, there has been *semantic change*, that is, words have altered in meaning. This is one of the greatest difficulties in reading the literature of the past; when we read Shakespeare, it is easy enough to remember that *presently* means "immediately" or that *to fear* may mean "to frighten"; it is a little harder to respond accurately to such words as *precise* ("puritanical"); and extremely difficult to get the exact force in any given context of a word with a wide range of connotations, like *temper* or *nature* or *blood*: to an Elizabethan, *blood* (for example) had various connotations connected with the passions, with high birth, with blood-relationship, and with vitality, and these rested on Renaissance theories of psychology, physiology, and social order. Change of meaning can be especially tricky when the general purport of the word has remained the same, but its range of meaning and its implications have changed. Sometimes, on the other hand, the change of meaning in a word over a long period can be sufficiently startling: to-day, the word *wan* means "pale," but in Anglo-Saxon times it meant "dark."

The third kind of change is in the inflexions of words (the endings of verbs and nouns, for example), or in the different grammatical forms of a word (*e.g.*, the form *men* as the dative singular of *man* in the King Alfred passage); this we can call *morphological change*. In this field there have been enormous changes in English in the last thousand years, as the language has shed most of the case-endings and other inflexions that once characterised it.

The fourth kind of change is in the way words can be put together in sentences—constructions, word-order, and so on. This we can call *syntactic change*. English syntax has changed a good deal since the days of King Alfred: as the inflexions have been lost, speakers have had to find new ways of showing the relationships between the words in a sentence, and this has been done above all by means of word-order and by the use of "function-words" (prepositions, adverbs, auxiliary verbs, etc.).

But there is a fifth kind of linguistic change which I have not yet mentioned, and an important one: *phonetic change*, or changes in the way the language is pronounced. Phonetic change in English is illustrated by the notorious discrepancy between our pronunciation and our spelling. Our present-day spellings were not really standardised until the eighteenth century, a great age for lexicographers and grammarians, but the spellings which then became more or less fixed were already very old, and represent, in the main, the pronunciation of English in the late Middle Ages. As an example we can take the word *light*, which appears in two of the four passages; in Chaucer's time, the *-gh-* in this word still represented a consonant-sound, and Chaucer's pronunciation of the word was probably quite close to the modern German pronunciation of the word *Licht*; however, this consonant-sound was already beginning to disappear in Chaucer's own day, although it was not finally lost from educated speech until the early seventeenth century; moreover, the vowel-sound in the word had also been changing, becoming a diphthong, and the early seventeenth-century pronunciation of *light* was probably something like the present-day pronunciation of the word *late*; during the seventeenth century, the sound of this diphthong developed further and the present-day pronunciation was reached in educated speech by about 1700. There are also words, however, where the spelling gives no such indication of changed pronunciation, but where we know on good evidence that sound-changes have taken place. As an example of this, we can take the words *dull* and *dullard*, which occur in the first two passages; the eighteenth-century author will have pronounced these words exactly as in educated south-eastern speech in England to-day, but in Elizabeth I's time the vowel-sound that we use in these words did not exist in educated English, and the sound that she used was like that in present-day *pull*. All words which we to-day pronounce with the *dull*-vowel were then pronounced with the *pull*-vowel; the change to the present pronunciation took place in the seventeenth century.

Besides illustrating the kinds of change that have taken place, the four passages also suggest its varying pace: the first passage, written a century and three-quarters ago, differs hardly at all from present-day usage; whereas the second and third passages (Queen Elizabeth's and Chaucer's), which are separated by an interval not much greater, are profoundly different from one another. The existence of periods of more rapid and deep-reaching change makes it convenient to divide the history of the language into certain broad periods. It is usual to divide it into three such periods: *Old English* (O.E.) is the name given to the language from the earliest Anglo-Saxon settlements in this country up to about the year 1100; from 1100 to about 1500 it is called *Middle English* (M.E.); and from 1500 to the present day *New English* (N.E.) or *Modern English* (MOD.E.). The King Alfred passage is therefore in Old English, the Chaucer passage in Middle English, and the other two in New English. These periods can also be subdivided, but this does not concern us here, except that it is convenient to have a term for the language as it exists in our own time; this I shall call *Present-day English* (P.E.).

All the kinds of change which we have noticed in the earlier periods of the language are still going on. It is surprising how many people think of linguistic change as something belonging to the past, something that took place in the age of Shakespeare, or in Middle English, or in Old English; and then, of course, it was quite respectable. When they meet an example of linguistic change in Present-day English, they use a different word for it: it is vulgar, or careless, or ungrammatical, or uneducated. In fact they become moralists or prescriptionists, intent on telling us how we ought to talk rather than contemplating with detachment the processes going on in the language to-day.

The prevalence of the prescriptive attitude in present-day England is illustrated by the prestige of the book which (significantly enough) is generally known simply as "Fowler." Its full title is *A Dictionary of Modern English Usage*, by H. W. Fowler, which is in fact a trifle ludicrous, for while it is true that Fowler quotes large numbers of examples of contemporary usage, he almost invariably does so in order to condemn them, to say that they are *not* acceptable usage. It is a strange kind of dictionary which collects its examples and then says what they ought to have been. Moreover, Fowler was writing nearly half a century ago, and some of the usages that he condemns have in the meantime become even more firmly established, so that a reading of his book gives one a clear idea of changes that have been going on in the language during that half-century; though that was certainly not his intention. This is not to deny that Fowler is good reading: he is perceptive, and often witty. But his book is certainly not, as its title seems to claim, a work of scientific description; it has, indeed, been described as "a set of prejudices erected into a system."

But the kind of linguistic conservatism seen in Fowler is a necessary part of any culture. There are always forces making for change in a language, and some resistance to it is necessary if the language is to be reasonably stable: we do not, after all, want to be incomprehensible to our grandchildren. Most of us, therefore, will find that we share some of Fowler's linguistic prejudices, perhaps a lot of them; I certainly do. I shudder, for example, when I hear *due to* used (as Fowler says) as "a mere compound preposition," where I should use "owing to" or "because of"; on the other hand, it is quite clear that this usage is now firmly established in this country (it is used regularly by the B.B.C.), and it is pointless and pedantic to make a fuss about it. In a way, we have to divide ourselves in two when we deal with the living language: as users of the language, we have to belong to some sub-group of the speech-community, and accept its standards, which we teach to our children: but as scientific observers we have to consider the usages of all such sub-groups impartially. So we are sometimes prescriptionists and sometimes observers.

When we adopt the scientific attitude of the observer and

describer of a language, there are two main approaches to choose between: either we can describe the language as it exists at a point in time, with no reference to the process by which it became what it is; or we can study the language historically, and see how it has changed with time. The second method, that of historical linguistics, was especially cultivated in the nineteenth century, and its great achievements tended to lead its practitioners to assume that the historical approach was the only valid one. This phase was ended about half a century ago, when Ferdinand de Saussure, in one of the great seminal books of twentieth-century linguistics, clearly pointed out the difference between the two methods, which he labelled the *synchronic* and the *diachronic*. The diachronic method is historical, the synchronic instantaneous. De Saussure also emphasised the idea of a language as a *system* (one of his favourite analogies was with a game of chess, where any move alters a whole system of relationships), and since his time a good deal of work has been done by the synchronic method to elucidate language-systems.

Now it might be thought that the ordinary user of a language is in the position of de Saussure's synchronic observer: he is aware of the language as a system which exists now, and its history is irrelevant to him. This is almost true, but not quite. It is not quite true because we all have memories, and are not merely aware of the language as it exists at the present moment, but also as it existed ten, twenty, perhaps fifty years ago; and moreover we are aware of differences between the language as it was then and as it is now. This is one of the reasons why we feel the language of some speakers (especially those older than ourselves) to be somewhat old-fashioned, while the language of others (especially those younger than ourselves) is felt to be lax and indecorous. For example, if somebody of a similar social and educational background to my own (and therefore with a similar style of speech) pronounces the word *often* with the same vowel as the word *law*, and talks about *an hotel* and *a motor-car* (instead of *a hotel* and *a car*), then I feel his speech as old-fashioned: but if he talks about *meeting up with* somebody (instead of just *meeting* them), and says *more common* (instead of *commoner*), and listens to the *radio* (instead of to the *wireless*), then I wonder what the younger generation is coming to. In practice, it is a whole set of such indications that makes one feel a man's speech as old-fashioned or neologistic: in a different style of speech, the pronunciation of *often* with a long vowel might simply be a sign of regional dialect, and have nothing to do with age. Again, when we read a play written twenty or thirty years ago, we often remark that the dialogue has *dated*: but it would hardly occur to us to say that the dialogue of an Elizabethan play has dated; the kinds of change involved in the language becoming dated are the kind we can remember, or imagine, taking place in our own lifetime, the kind of difference between old-fashioned and new-fashioned speech.

Our consciousness of such differences is not only due to our memory of the language in the past: a part is no doubt also played by our observations in the present of the speech-behaviour of different groups: the young notice that the old speak differently from themselves, and this observation alone will be enough to give rise to the concept of old-fashioned speech. But the older we get, the more we become aware of the changes actually taking place in our lifetime. At the same time, our own speech changes, and to some extent we are aware of this; at the very least we are aware that some of the words that we use are new ones: sputniks and beatniks have the conscious charm of novelty.

Because we all have this first-hand experience of linguistic change, the study of the living language is a good way of embarking on historical linguistics. The living language is in any case the best starting-point for all linguistic study: the student should begin by listening to his own speech, and the speech of the people around him, and trying to analyse it. This would be an attempt at a synchronic analysis: but there is no reason why the diachronic study of language should not also begin from the living language. This book is a modest attempt to help the student to begin in this way, by giving an account of the changes that have been going on in our own memories and which will probably continue in the immediate future. Since any change takes time to manifest itself, I shall constantly be comparing the language as it is to-day with the language as it was ten years ago, twenty years ago, and even (since many changes are gradual) fifty years ago.

There are pretty obvious difficulties in this undertaking; if it were to be done thoroughly, it would involve large-scale investigations by a team of specialists, repeated at intervals of a few years: but this is hardly likely to be done. For the single observer, it is difficult to see the wood for the trees, and I have certainly made mistakes of emphasis and missed things of importance: but this does not very much matter if the reader is stimulated to look and listen for himself, for most of the things that I shall discuss can be observed by the reader himself in his own speech-environment.

The reader who does listen attentively to the language over a period of years will probably agree that quite a lot of change is going on in it. This is especially noticeable in the vocabulary, which in the last few years has acquired a good many new words, but it can also be seen in pronunciation, syntax, and the meanings of words. The chapters that follow will deal separately with (*a*) the changing relationship between the different dialects, (*b*) phonetic change, (*c*) the growth of the vocabulary, (*d*) semantic change, and (*e*) changes in syntax and morphology. I shall confine myself to a consideration of the English spoken in England, but much of what I say will certainly be true for the whole of the United Kingdom, and some of it will be true for the rest of the English-speaking world.

Chapter I:

Notes and suggestions for further reading

I shall not attempt to give detailed references for all the topics I discuss, but at the end of each chapter I shall make suggestions for further reading, so that the reader can, if he wishes, follow up various lines of thought suggested in the chapter. Some of these will be elementary books, but I shall also mention more advanced books, and detailed monographs on specialised topics which will interest the serious student but not the amateur.

The beginner who is interested in linguistics generally might well start with Simeon Potter's Pelican book, *Language in the Modern World* (1960); the same author's *Modern Linguistics* (London 1957) is a little more advanced. The work of F. de Saussure's referred to in the text is *Cours de linguistique générale* (Paris 1916), which is also available in English translation. Other twentieth-century classics are Edward Sapir, *Language* (New York 1921), and Leonard Bloomfield, *Language* (New York 1933). Useful books for the student are L. R. Palmer, *An Introduction to Modern Linguistics* (London 1936); E. H. Sturtevant, *An Introduction to Linguistic Science* (New Haven 1947); H. A. Gleason, *An Introduction to Descriptive Linguistics* (New York 1955); and C. F. Hockett, *A Course in Modern Linguistics* (New York 1958). The most influential English linguist in the present century has been the late J. R. Firth, but his influence has been spread more by his direct teaching to his own pupils than by his publications; the serious student, however, should read his *Studies in Linguistic Analysis* (Oxford 1957).

Those who are interested in the history of the English language can well begin with my own Pan piper, *The Story of Language* (London 1964), or with Simeon Potter, *Our Language* (1950), or with G. L. Brook, *A History of the English Language* (London 1958), or with C. L. Wrenn, *The English Language* (London 1949). Other elementary books, older but still useful, are H. Bradley, *The Making of English* (London 1904), and O. Jespersen, *Growth and Structure of the English Language* (Oxford 1905). More detailed treatments will be found in A. C. Baugh, *History of the English Language* (2nd edn., London 1959), and in Stuart Robertson, *The Development of Modern English* (2nd edn., revised by F. G. Cassidy, New York 1954). H. C. Wyld, *A Short History of English* (3rd edn., London 1927), deals mainly with phonology. A detailed work for the student, which had only been carried as far as the early New English period when its author died, is Karl Luick's *Historische Grammatik der Englischen Sprache* (Leipzig 1914-21).

An introduction to the history of Modern English is provided by J. Wright and E. M. Wright, *An Elementary Historical New English Grammar* (Oxford 1924), which deals especially with phonology. For the student, there is Otto Jespersen's massive work *A Modern English Grammar on Historical Principles*, 7 vols. (1909-49, Heidelberg I-IV, London V-VI and Copenhagen VII), a large part of which is devoted to syntax. Other books on Modern English include H. A. Poutsma, *A Grammar of Late Modern English* (Groningen 1914-26); E. A. Kruisinga, *A Handbook of Present-Day English* (Utrecht 1925-32); G. O. Curme and H. Kurath, *A Grammar of the English Language*, vols. 2 and 3 (Boston 1931-5); and R. W. Zandvoort, *A Handbook of English Grammar* (London 1957). The best book on the grammar of present-day British English is Barbara M. H. Strang, *Modern English Structure* (London 1962). Good descriptions of the structure of present-day American English are given by Paul Roberts,

Patterns of English (New York 1956) (very elementary), by W. Nelson Francis, *The Structure of American English* (New York 1958), and by A. A. Hill, *Introduction to Linguistic Structures* (New York 1958); however, the student who has British English as his mother tongue (or the overseas student who has learnt British English) would be well advised to defer reading these three books until he has done some solid reading on British usage, and especially on the phonetics of British English, as otherwise he may become confused. Many of the books mentioned in the first half of this paragraph now look rather old-fashioned; however, a programme of analysis on Present-day English has been started at University College, London, under the direction of Professor Randolph Quirk, and it is to be hoped that this will soon begin providing us with up-to-date descriptions of British usage.

I know of no book dealing specifically with linguistic change in Present-day English, though the final chapters of many histories of the English language point to a number of things that are going on. In addition to the histories already mentioned, see F. Mossé, *Esquisse d'une histoire de la langue anglaise* (Lyon 1947), an elementary book which has an interesting chapter on recent developments. There are also many suggestive comments on current developments in Ernst Leisi, *Das heutige Englisch* (Heidelberg 1955), a book designed for German students of English.

The only learned periodical which devotes itself wholly to the living language is *American Speech*, published quarterly by the Columbia University Press. Another periodical which, while covering the whole field of English language and literature, has quite frequent articles on the living language is *English Studies*, published every two months in Amsterdam. Especially valuable for the teacher of English as a foreign language is the British Council's periodical *English Language Teaching*, published quarterly in London; it has regular discussions on points of current usage.

The four passages quoted in the text as examples of linguistic change are all taken from translations of Boethius's *De consolatione philosophiae*; from a puristic standpoint, therefore, they cannot be taken as absolutely reliable examples of the usage of their times, as they may have been influenced in varying degrees by their Latin original (*e.g.*, in word-order and constructions); they are useful for a brief elementary demonstration, however, as they show four writers of different periods tackling exactly the same material. The first passage is from the translation by the Rev. Philip Ridpath, published in London in 1785. The second is from the translation by Queen

Elizabeth I, taken from the volume published by the Early English Text Society called *Queen Elizabeth's Englishings*, ed. Caroline Pemberton (London 1899). The third is from Geoffrey Chaucer's version; I have taken my text from the E.E.T.S. edition, ed. Richard Morris (London 1868). The fourth is from King Alfred's translation, ed. W. J. Sedgefield (Oxford 1899). I give Ridpath's version exactly as published; Queen Elizabeth's version I have modernised in spelling and punctuation; in the Chaucer, I have modernised the punctuation, replaced the obsolete letters ʒ and þ by appropriate modern ones, and modernised the use of *i* and *j*, *u* and *v*; the only changes I have made in the King Alfred passage are to expand the abbreviations for *and* and *that*, and to change *goode* to the more usual *gode*.

The early seventeenth-century pronunciation of *light* was probably [ləit] rather than [leit], but I have not gone into this in the text, since I have not yet introduced phonetic symbols (for which, see Chapter III).

The account given in the text of the history of the *do*-forms is based on the conclusions reached by Alvar Ellegård in his monograph on the subject, *The Auxiliary Do: the Establishment and Regulation of its Use in English* (Stockholm 1953), but I have simplified a little.

Chapter II

Standard English and Dialect

ONE way in which the English language has been changing in recent years is in the relationship between the different kinds of English spoken in England, and in people's attitudes to these different varieties of the language. On the one hand, there has been a trend towards greater uniformity, a levelling out of differences; on the other hand, there has been an increased reluctance to accept as a norm what has hitherto been considered the standard form of the spoken language. In sum the effect has been to make the language more mixed.

It is obvious to all of us that different kinds of English are spoken, even inside England. This is not merely a question of individual peculiarities (though these of course exist), but of the peculiarities of *groups* of speakers. We can all recognise a kind of speech characteristic of the north of England, of the West Country, and of the London area, even if we lack the power to analyse the differences; in other words there are in England clearly marked *regional dialects*, and these are much more numerous and finely graded than is apparent to the untrained ear; the ordinary Londoner recognises a style of speech as "northern," but he is in fact lumping together a whole host of dialects; the speech of Lancashire differs from that of Yorkshire, that of the West Riding from that of the East Riding, and so on; and within these areas there are even finer differences, between districts, between towns, sometimes even between neighbouring villages; though in real life you will never meet a dialectologist who can, like Professor Higgins in Shaw's *Pygmalion*, distinguish between the dialects of different streets. To the ordinary speaker, the most obvious differences between the regional dialects are those of pronunciation: the Londoner trying to imitate Lancashire speech will usually concentrate on such things as the vowel-sounds in the words *cup* and *ask* and *don't*, and (if he is a good mimic) on certain distinctive features of rhythm and melody. But there are also differences in vocabulary ("dialect words") and grammar. "If t'United had less brass to lake wi', they'd lake better fooitball," says one of Mr J. B. Priestley's Yorkshire characters, using words that would be strange (and even incomprehensible) in the south. "I nivver reckoned nowt o' barbers," says another, using a construction equally alien to the southerner.

Besides being thus diversified horizontally into regional dialects, the language is also diversified vertically, into *class dialects*. In a given town, the mill-hand, the clerk, the primary-school teacher, the shopkeeper, the lawyer, the bank-manager, and the company-director may all speak a local variant of the language, but they will also speak a sub-variant of it, according to their social status, social pretensions, and education. In every district there is a hierarchy of dialects, corresponding in some degree with the local social structure. A speaker will tend to find that the speech of people lower down in this hierarchy sounds "rough" or "vulgar" (and perhaps also picturesque); while the speech of people higher in the scale will sound either affected ("posh") or desirably refined, according to his ambitions and social orientation. Such judgments have little to do with any intrinsic quality of the language, but are simply due to association: if by some historical accident the vowel-sounds of the Cockney and of the Eton boy had been distributed to them the other way round, we should still have found the speech of the Cockney "vulgar" and that of the Eton boy "posh."

The social stratification of the language appears in syntax and vocabulary as well as in pronunciation. The speaker higher in the scale describes many of the usages of lower strata as "ungrammatical": it would be more accurate to say that the grammar of these dialects is different from the grammar of his own. In vocabulary, one can sometimes find a whole series of words used at different social levels: a good example of this is the word for the course of a meal which follows the main course; there are regional variations in this, but the general pattern of usage is as follows: _pudding_ (upper and upper-middle), _sweet_ (middle), _dessert_ (lower-middle), _afters_ (lower-middle and lower), and _pudding_ (lower). The coincidence in usage between top and bottom is interesting, and is found in some other things.

Such differences are often marked by referring to the speech as "educated" and "uneducated"; to some extent, "education" is here merely a euphemism for "class," for, although class has for centuries been a topic of the greatest interest in England (as the novel reveals), our own age seems to find the subject a trifle indelicate, and only to be referred to indirectly (like sex, war, death, lavatories, and economic depressions). However, "education" in this context is not _only_ a euphemism for class, for it is in fact true that our style of speech is affected by our education. This can often be seen where members of the same family have been through different parts of the educational machine: one may have left school at fourteen and gone into the mill; a second may have gone through grammar school and got a job in business; while a third may have won a scholarship to Oxford and ended up in one of the learned professions; even if they make no conscious effort to adapt their speech to their _milieu_ (which of course many of them do), such sets of siblings will end up with markedly different styles of speech, simply from the influence of their varying speech-environments. But even here, of course, there is a close correlation between education and class, since different educations lead to different occupations; not many university graduates are content, like Jimmy Porter, to become barrow-boys.

The regional dialects show the greatest differences from one another at the bottom of the hierarchy, because of the relative immobility of the working classes, and their more limited contacts; as you move up the scale, the regional differences diminish, so that the difference between educated speakers from, say, London, Manchester, and Gloucester may be quite slight. In other words, "the lower the broader." Indeed, at the very top of the social scale regional differences disappear altogether, and we reach what English people often call "standard English" or "the Queen's English"; I shall call it "Received Standard."

I am suggesting, then, that one change taking place in Present-day English is that these dialectal differences are being reduced; both regional and class dialects are still clearly marked but the range of difference is getting less. One reason for this is the increased mobility of the population, as a result of improved communications. Local dialect differences develop and persist most easily in a settled and relatively closed and self-contained community. But the whole development of England since the Industrial Revolution has been away from the settled and self-contained local community, and so has been hostile to regional dialect differentiation. One symptom of this is seen in the way in which the traditional rural dialects are dying out. The Dialect Survey of England, carried out from headquarters in the University of Leeds, has collected precious historical material on the rural dialects only just in time; in a few more years it would have been lost for ever. One difficulty for the field-workers on the Survey was that they could not trust the authenticity of a dialect speaker unless he had always lived in the same place; if he had spent ten years of his life in a neighbouring industrial city, or had travelled the world in the armed forces, then he could not be used. This is a clear illustration of the way in which better communications and greater physical mobility are levelling out dialect differences.

In the present century, this levelling trend has been enormously reinforced by two further factors: the mass-media and popular education. These things have been operating for over half a century: the modern type of popular newspaper goes back to the *Daily Mail* of the eighteen-nineties, and the final establishment of universal and compulsory education to about the same period: but their influence has steadily increased as the older generation has died out, and it has been successively reinforced by that of the cinema, of the wireless, and now of television. The mass-media do not, of course, change a Manchester dialect speaker into a London dialect speaker: but they do encourage a standardisation of vocabulary (so that *traffic-lights* are gaining ground at the expense of *robots*) and of syntax (so that "Wait while I come" is sinking in the social scale, as "Wait till I come" diffuses outwards and downwards). As far as pronunciation is concerned, they probably work against the "broadest" pronunciations, so that all speakers tend to move upwards in the local pronunciation hierarchy, thus reducing its total range; some distinctive local features of pronunciation, like the Northumberland "burr," seem to be dying out. The effect of the school is similar and often deliberate; a few schools adopt the policy of not interfering with their pupils' dialect, but even these pupils are hardly likely to escape being influenced by the speech of their teachers and the language of their text-books.

However, the influence of the mass-media and of mass-education, while working against the broader dialect elements, does not necessarily produce speakers of Received Standard English. Most primary-school teachers, and a large number of grammar-school teachers, are not themselves speakers of Received Standard, and their effect on their pupils is to tone down the broader dialect elements (both in pronunciation and in idiom) without removing regional characteristics altogether. On the wireless and on television, a good deal of Received Standard is heard, but is not necessarily the most influential form of speech. B.B.C. announcers may be less influential than comedians, quizmasters, compères, and "personalities," many of whom have regional accents; for some of them, indeed, the accent is an important part of the personality: part of the appeal of Mr Wilfred Pickles, for example, surely lies in his educated Yorkshire speech, with its suggestions of forthrightness, homeliness, common sense, and a heart of gold (qualities that we know all Yorkshiremen possess).

Another thing about the mass-media which works against Received Standard is the large amount of American speech that is heard—in the cinema, on the wireless and television, and on records of pop-singers (and English pop-singers have developed a special pseudo-American accent of their own). In some sections of the English community there is strong resistance to American speech-habits, especially among older members of the upper classes and perhaps among schoolteachers (ever in favour of undefiled wells): but other sections, especially adolescents and those under the spell of the entertainments industry, are extremely receptive, and there is a steady filtering-in of American words and phrases. Many of these merely push British English a bit further along the way it's already going: a phrase like *meet up with* instead of the simple *meet* illustrates a process already going on in Britain and America alike, namely the development of phrases consisting of a verb followed by adverbs or prepositions (to get across somebody, to fix somebody up with something, to put up with something, to get on well with somebody, to get away with something, to laugh something off, etc.). On the other hand, some American forms are alien to us: *spark-plug* and *long-play record* and *frypan* illustrate compounds not natural in this country (where we say *sparking-plug*, *long-playing record* and *frying-pan*); if they become established here, they may start a new fashion: recently I have seen *four-seat saloon* in an English book, and *swim-pool* in a high-class newspaper. Despite the extent to which adolescents try to put on American accents, I do not think that this is having much effect on British pronunciation. If there is any effect, it is more likely to be on the pronunciation (and especially the stressing) of single words, than on the entire sound-pattern of the language. I should certainly be glad if we could adopt the American stressing of *temporarily*: pronounced our way, it is an awful tongue-twister, and is often reduced to *temporally* (which may of course prove to be the long-term solution).

This American influence on British speech may perhaps seem to run counter to the trend I have been discussing, that is, the increasing uniformity of the language inside England. It is possible, however, that it is rather an example of the same thing happening on a larger scale: with the great increase in world-wide communications, it is probable that the various forms of English spoken in the world are now influencing one another more than formerly, and that the trend to greater dialectal mixing is therefore taking place in English on a world scale. As far as America and Britain are concerned, it is obvious that the influence is almost wholly one of America on Britain, not *vice versa*; in this, as in other ways, the U.S. is a creditor nation.

In discussing the changes going on in Present-day British English, I shall not try to distinguish too closely between native developments and American imports. It is in any case often difficult to distinguish between them, since many developments in the two languages are parallel: it sometimes happens, for example, that an American usage which is imported into educated British speech already exists in British dialects, or is simply a more advanced stage of something already happening in educated British speech. This is one of the reasons why many Americanisms have been so thoroughly assimilated into British English in the present century that we are no longer conscious of them as Americanisms at all.

The second main trend that I wish to discuss is the increasing resistance to what has hitherto been accepted as Standard English. By this I do not mean the accepted written language, standard literary English, which is written by many people who are not speakers of Received Standard, but a certain recognised standard of spoken English, towards which many people have striven in the past century or more. However, I am referring not only to pronunciation, although this is a distinctive part of Received Standard, but also to vocabulary and idiom; when I wish to refer to pronunciation alone, I shall call it Received Pronunciation (r.p.), whereas I shall use the expression Received Standard (r.s.) to refer to all aspects of the language.

Received Standard is the language of the English gentry. It is interesting as an example of a class dialect which is not also a regional dialect; it is of course a regional dialect from the point of view of the English-speaking world as a whole, but inside England it is non-regional, and is spoken by members of the upper classes whatever part of the country they come from. It must go back historically to some variant of a regional dialect —presumably, like the literary language, to the East-Midland dialect of late Middle English (with certain border influences from other dialects): but to-day it has no local place, but is propagated within the family, and above all in the school, the upper-class boarding school.

Indeed, the dominance of this non-regional dialect among the upper classes probably coincides with the period of the dominance of the public school in their education, that is, roughly since the time of Arnold of Rugby in the early Victorian age; it is true that the differentiation between grammar school and public school is visible as early as the seventeenth century, and becomes wide in the eighteenth century, but both types of school were going through a bad period at that time, and many of the rich had their children educated at home by private tutors; it is in the nineteenth century that the public school really comes into its own as *the* form of upper-class education, and the dominance of a non-regional upper-class speech probably goes back to the same period. It is true that before this time there was a prestige dialect, that of the Court and of London society, but it had nothing like the universal acceptance among the English gentry that Received Standard has had in recent times. George Puttenham, writing in 1589, advises the poet to avoid regional dialect:

> neither shall he take the termes of Northern-men, such as they use in dayly talke, whether they be noble men or gentlemen, or of their best clarkes all is a matter: nor in effect any speach used beyond the river of Trent, though no man can deny but that theirs is the purer English Saxon at this day, yet it is not so Courtly nor so currant as our Southerne English is, no more is the far Westerne mans speach: ye shall therefore take the usuall speach of the Court, and that of London and the shires lying about London within lx. miles, and not much above.

Puttenham hastens to add that of course there are gentlemen and others in every shire who can speak, and especially write, as good southern English as anybody: but it is clear from the passage quoted above that he would quite expect northern gentlemen and scholars and even northern noblemen to speak a regional form of the language. It rather sounds from the passage, too, as though Puttenham would also have expected regional dialect from a gentleman from the West Country; and it is notable that Sir Walter Raleigh, that accomplished courtier, retained his West-Country accent throughout his life. In the seventeenth and eighteenth centuries, too, many country gentlemen spoke a regional dialect, as the drama and the novel testify: the contrast between Witwoud and his cousin Sir Wilful in Congreve's *Way of the World*, or between Squire Allworthy and Squire Western in Fielding's *Tom Jones*, is not one between gentry and non-gentry, but between the gentleman who has town-breeding and the one who is a country bumpkin.

The importance of the public school in the propagation of Received Pronunciation is recognised by Professor Daniel Jones in his *Pronouncing Dictionary of English*, which he claims is a record of the pronunciation of people educated at public schools. Jones, however, also gives his group a regional basis, for he says that he is recording the pronunciation usually heard "in the families of Southern English people who have been educated at the public schools." I think that it would be possible to dispense with this regional criterion, provided that one made the list of schools sufficiently select; and Jones himself, in his *Phonetics of English*, says that the pronunciation in public and preparatory schools is "fairly uniform" and is "independent of their locality." Jones gives no definition of a public school: he obviously does not mean to include all Headmasters' Conference schools, for many of these, in whatever part of England, produce predominantly non-standard speakers. If challenged, he would probably define the public school by giving a list.

Received Standard has had great prestige, and people rising in the social scale have tended to try to acquire it. The difficulties of this task have led to intermediate dialects, such as the variety of English which may be described as the Suburban Genteel, and the laid-on-with-a-trowel variety often attributed (no doubt unjustly) to Kensington. The situation has also led to the recognition of many linguistic class-indicators (napkin/serviette, lavatory/toilet, pudding/sweet/dessert/afters, etc.), which have been stumbling blocks to the parvenu. Linguistic snobbery has been an enduring feature of the English cultural landscape (as of that of many other countries, of course).

Now it seems to me that, during the last half century and especially since the Second World War, this mode of speech has lost some of its prestige, and is losing its once unchallenged position as the "correct" way to talk. There are many reasons for this, no doubt, but among them are certainly social and political ones; above all, the speech of the gentry has declined in prestige because of the decline of the gentry themselves: with the rise of democracy in England, and much greater equality of opportunity, they have lost a good deal of their former privileged status. I don't want to overstate this: a public-school education still has very great prestige and pull, and Eton is still the surest path to the Foreign Office; there are still large regions in business and industry where the right school plus the right pronunciation will get you further than a science degree

from a redbrick university plus the wrong pronunciation; and
there are still people on the up-and-up who are trying to get
rid of their northern vowels or their western r-sound, who are
practising saying pudding and napkin and lavatory, who are
trying to make *brass* rhyme with *farce* (or better still changing it
to *money*). But there has been a change, especially in the last
fifteen years, for Eton is no longer the only path to the Foreign
Office; ex-elementary-school boys become cabinet-ministers;
and there are many men of the professional classes who, far
from practising the sounds of R.P. and the prestige-words of R.S.,
are deliberately refusing to do so.

An important part in this has been played by the changes in
the educational system. Before the War, despite all the variety
in English education, it was essentially a three-tier system: the
elementary schools for the lower classes, the grammar schools
for the middle classes, and the public schools for the upper
classes; there was a so-called "educational ladder" which en-
abled the bright child to move up to a higher part of the system,
but "ladder" is a fair description of its width. The 1944 Education Act in effect threw open the grammar schools to the
brighter children of the working classes, by competitive examination. The system is fiercely competitive and the number of
places is limited, but still it is true to-day that the really talented
and determined child of working-class origins can and will get
to a grammar school. And, with the vast expansion of university education since the War, and the great increase in the
number of scholarships (now held by about 80 per cent of university students), the really able grammar-school pupil of any
social background can get to the university. This means that
people entering the professional classes to-day come from lower
in the social scale, on the average, than before the War, and
in fact considerable numbers of young men and women of
working-class or lower-middle-class origins are coming out of
the universities to become civil servants, lawyers, doctors,
teachers, and so on. About one-third of university students
to-day are the children of manual workers; many more are the
children of lower-grade clerical workers, small shopkeepers, and
so on. Consequently, the majority of university students to-day
are not speakers of Received Standard; among the students

that I myself teach, in the Arts Faculty of an extremely respectable provincial university (which draws its students from
all over the country), not one student in ten speaks R.S., probably not one in twenty. No doubt the ratio is very much higher
at Oxford and Cambridge, which still draw proportionately
more of their students from the public schools: but Oxford and
Cambridge account for a smaller part of our university population than before the War, and their share in it (at present
about one-sixth) will continue to fall as expansion continues.

A surprisingly large number of this new intelligentsia are
apparently quite indifferent about R.P., showing little sign of
being either snobs or inverted snobs about it. But, interestingly
enough, there is also a substantial section which is positively
hostile to it. This is not entirely new, of course, for while Received Standard has always produced deference in some people,
it has equally caused hostility in others, especially among the
industrial working classes. One of the first linguistic facts that
many of us must have noticed when we passed through the
ranks at the beginning of the last War was the speed and unan-
imity with which a barrack-room would react against anybody
thought to be putting on linguistic airs ("talking posh" or
"talking la-di-da"); officers of course were different—they were
expected to talk like that—though an officer with a particularly
marked upper-class accent was always liable to be mimicked
behind his back (especially if disliked for other reasons). This
kind of hostility seems now to be appearing among the professional classes, among the new intelligentsia produced by the
educational and social changes of the last few years.

Their resentment at Received Standard is no doubt fed by
various other resentments: a sense of frustration, a feeling that
others have unfair advantages, feelings of social inferiority, a
rejection of Old Gang politics, in fact general resentment at the
Establishment (itself a significant new post-war concept). It is
these resentments that have led to the phrase "the angry young
men." This of course has been used as a blanket-phrase to
cover a large number of different phenomena, but the original
angry young man, Jimmy Porter in John Osborne's play *Look
Back in Anger*, is in fact a clear example of the new type of graduate, the working-class boy who has made his career through

the grammar school and university: and what he is most angry about is the upper classes, especially as embodied in his wife's relations. Another example of the New Intellectual is the hero of Kingsley Amis's *Lucky Jim*, a redbrick graduate whose opposition to the Establishment takes the form of a calculated philistinism; and a third is the hero of John Braine's novel *Room at the Top*, a book which, for all its deficiencies, gives a remarkable picture of class-feelings in the changing class-structure of postwar England, and of the corrupting power of the society which produces those feelings. The great success of these three works with the English public shows the extent to which they are canalising current feelings; the new working-class intellectual and his resentment at the Establishment are certainly realities of our time. And this resentment can also be directed at Received Standard as the language of the Establishment.

The upshot is that there are many educated people to-day who do not speak Received Standard, and many of them don't want to. Such people usually speak the educated form of the regional dialect, which can be called Regional Standard; this cannot be defined as accurately as Received Standard, since there is a considerable spread downwards, but in each region there is a certain range at the top of the speech-hierarchy within which the speech of an educated man (*e.g.*, a man with a university degree or equivalent qualification) is likely to fall. This is not an entirely new situation; especially in Yorkshire and Lancashire, with their strong local pride and their contempt for the cissy south, there has long been a tendency to feel the local standard as (at least) the equal of Received Standard: but this feeling is now far more widespread, and stronger, and the people who hold it are becoming increasingly important in the community.

There are many possible ways in which this situation could develop, and a good deal depends on the social history of England in the coming years. Perhaps the rebels of to-day will be absorbed into the upper classes of to-morrow like so many New Men of the past (sixteenth-century clothiers, nineteenth-century captains of industry, twentieth-century trade-union leaders), and Received Standard will reassert itself, though modified by the incomers. Or perhaps there will be such profound social changes that R.S. will actually become an undesirable form of speech, which people try to conceal, like upper-class Russian after the Bolshevik Revolution; though there seems little sign at the moment of a development in this direction. Or perhaps some intermediate line of social development will lead to the acceptance of all the Regional Standards as of equal status with R.S. Educated Northern English (mainly Yorkshire and Lanca-shire) is especially influential, because of the great northern industrial centres, and in particular is spoken by large numbers of scientists and technicians; and it is not impossible that we shall end up with two Standards, a northern and a southern. What is perhaps most likely, however, because it is what is actually happening at the moment, is that one of the regional standards will come to be recognised as a new national stan-dard, perhaps coalescing with the present R.S. in the process. The regional standard which is taking on this role is that of the most populous and influential part of England, London and the south-east, which of all the regional standards is the one closest to R.S. (so much so, indeed, that many people cannot distinguish between them). Many people, if asked to define Received Standard English, would in fact define it as the speech of the educated classes of the south-east of England, and not, as I have done, as the speech of the English gentry. The older idea of R.S. no doubt persists most strongly among people edu-cated at public schools, to whom south-eastern Regional Stan-dard still sounds sub-standard: but there is an increasing body of speakers who have not been to public schools but who regard themselves as speakers of R.S.

In this book I shall deal with the changes going on in the language of educated people in England: in other words I shall be considering the various regional standards as well as R.S. When I deal with pronunciation, however, I shall confine my-self to R.P. and the educated speech of south-eastern England: it would be impossible in a short book to deal with the phono-logy of all the regions, even if I were competent to do so.

Because of the change which is going on in the concept of *standard English*, and because of the social changes of the post-war period, some of the linguistic changes which we shall note will be changes in acceptance, rather than changes in actual usage. Usages which are not new, but which have previously been considered non-standard, are now coming to be accepted as standard by increasing numbers of educated speakers (though not always by the speaker of R.S. proper). Whenever possible, I shall try to indicate whether a development in the language involves a new usage, or only an acceptance of a variant form already in existence.

A few years ago, public attention was drawn to the question of standard and non-standard speech, and two new terms were coined: *U* and *non-U*. The coiner was Professor Alan Ross, who in 1954 published in a Finnish learned journal an article called "Linguistic class-indicators in present-day English." Ross sets out from the premise that English society is tripartite in structure, with an upper, middle, and lower class. A linguistic usage which is acceptable to the upper class he denotes by the symbol U; one which is not acceptable to the upper-class is non-U. On this definition, U-usage should be identical with Received Standard as I have defined it.

Ross discusses many aspects of U-usage: pronunciation, stress, vocabulary, phrases, how to address an envelope, or an archbishop, and so on. A very large number of the usages that he describes as non-U would also be unacceptable in the Regional Standards, and especially in that of the south-east. But there are some usages which he describes as non-U which are certainly acceptable in most or all of the Regional Standard forms of the language. I will give a few examples of these, taken from the sphere of vocabulary. According to Ross, it is non-U to say that people are *cultivated* or *cultured*; shockingly enough, there is no U-equivalent for this usage, though *civilised* might be possible. It is non-U to talk about a *cruet* or a *dress-suit*, to say *mirror* (instead of *looking-glass*), or to use *notepaper* (instead of *writing-paper*). Moreover, a member of the upper classes is never *wealthy* (always *rich*), never uses *toilet-paper* (only *lavatory-paper*) and never listens to the *radio* (always to the *wireless*). The non-U alternatives in these examples are certainly used widely among the educated classes in England.

This article was brought to the notice of the public by Miss Nancy Mitford, in *Encounter*, and led to a good deal of discussion. There are two interesting things to notice about this

discussion. The first is that the predominant reaction to the
whole business was one of amusement; no doubt some people
studied the various letters and articles published on the subject
in order to purge their speech of non-U elements, but this does
not seem to have been the common reaction; most people who
were interested treated the whole thing as a bit of a joke, and
turned it into a party-game. This in itself suggests that R.S. is
declining in prestige.

The second point is that there was great disagreement about
what in fact constitutes U-usage; many of Ross's analyses were
contradicted by people claiming to be undoubted members of
the upper classes who were in turn contradicted by others. One
reason for this, no doubt, is that there are sub-dialects within
U-speech: but another reason may well be that the standard is
breaking down and that there is widespread confusion about
what constitutes U-usage (and indeed about what constitutes
the upper classes). Ross himself was partly responsible for the
disagreement, for his original article provided no satisfactory
definition of the group whose usage he was claiming to describe.
At the beginning of his article, he says that the upper class in
England can no longer be distinguished from other classes by
its education, its wealth, its cleanliness, its occupations, its pastimes, or the part it plays in public life, and he finally concludes
that the only way of recognising a member of the upper class
to-day is by his speech. But this makes his whole argument
circular: he undertakes to describe to us the linguistic usage of
a group, and when asked to define the group he in effect says
"It's the people who speak in the way I'm going to describe."
This throws doubt on the validity of his analyses, since they
may be personal prejudice rather than objective description;
even if they do truly describe the usage of a group, it may only
be a sub-group of the upper classes, perhaps a sub-group to
which Professor Ross himself belongs; or it may be a group
which some people would say does not in fact belong to the
upper classes.

However, although this makes Ross's article somewhat un-
satisfactory, it is an interesting piece of evidence about the social
changes of our times and their effect on our attitude to language. In Edwardian and Victorian times, Ross implies, things

were quite different; then you could recognise a member of the
upper classes by all these other things—wealth, occupation,
pastimes, education, part played in public life, and so on—
besides his speech: but now he is rivalled in all these things by
people who speak differently. This obviously supports my general thesis that the decline of Received Standard in our time
has at least in part been caused by the decline of the English
gentry.

Chapter II:

Notes and suggestions for further reading

Puttenham's remarks about regional speech and the language of the
court can be found in *The Arte of English Poesie*, ed. Edward Arber
(London 1869), p. 157. My example of Sir Walter Raleigh as a
dialect-speaker is taken from H. C. Wyld, *A History of Modern
Colloquial English* (2nd edn., 1921), p. 103; Wyld has a good deal of
interest to say about regional and social dialect. Daniel Jones's *An
English Pronouncing Dictionary* was published in London in 1917,
and has since been through many editions, with additions and
corrections; I have used the eighth edition (1947), but I have also
made some use of earlier and later editions, since the changes that
Jones makes often reflect changes in pronunciation. Professor Ross's
article, "Linguistic class-indicators in present-day English," was
published in *Neuphilologische mitteilungen*, LV (1954), pp. 20-56; it was
reprinted, in a slightly simplified form, in *Noblesse Oblige*, ed. Nancy
Mitford (London 1956).

On the methods and problems of dialectology, see A. McIntosh,
An Introduction to a Survey of Scottish Dialects (Edinburgh 1952). A
useful historical introduction to the regional dialects of Britain is
W. W. Skeat's little book *English Dialects from the Eighth Century to
the Present Day* (Cambridge 1911). A more modern work, also suitable
for the beginner, is G. L. Brook's *English Dialects* (London 1963). A
standard work of reference is Joseph Wright's *English Dialect
Dictionary*, 6 vols. (London 1898-1905). There are also a number
of monographs by different writers on individual dialects. The work
on the English rural dialects referred to in the text has now begun to
appear in a series of volumes under the general title of *A Survey of
English Dialects*, by Harold Orton and Eugen Dieth (Leeds 1962-);
it is to be hoped that a similar survey will one day be undertaken
for the English urban dialects. The classical example of a linguistic

Chapter III

Changes in Pronunciation

IT is difficult to talk about pronunciation without going into technicalities to some extent, but I shall try not to use technical terms without giving at least some brief indication of their meaning. However, if you are at all interested in language you should have some knowledge of the science of phonetics, and at the end of the chapter I give some suggestions for reading on the subject; nobody can get far in language-study without such knowledge. But a word of warning: it is necessary to sharpen your ear as well as to learn phonetic theory; too often one meets foreign students of English whose theoretical knowledge of English phonetics is good, but whose pronunciation is abominable; and even if it is your native language that you are concerned with, it takes practice to correlate what you hear with the theory you have learnt.

Because of the discrepancies between spelling and pronunciation, I shall have to use a phonetic alphabet. The symbols I shall use, with words to illustrate their pronunciation, are given below; the illustrative words are given, first in normal spelling, then in my phonetic transcription.

List of Phonetic Symbols for English
(Received Pronunciation)

Pure Vowels

iː	as in *tree* (triː), *seize* (siːz), *people* (piːpl)
i	as in *sit* (sit), *examine* (igˈzæmin), *horses* (ˈhɔːsiz)
e	as in *pen* (pen), *deaf* (def), *tell* (tel)
æ	as in *cat* (kæt), *gas* (gæs)
ɑː	as in *far* (fɑː), *aunt* (ɑːnt), *half* (hɑːf)
ɔ	as in *hot* (hɔt), *sorry* (ˈsɔri), *want* (wɔnt)

ɔː	as in *saw* (sɔː), *form* (fɔːm), *all* (ɔːl)
u	as in *put* (put), *book* (buk)
uː	as in *do* (duː), *rule* (ruːl), *cube* (kjuːb)
ʌ	as in *cup* (kʌp), *come* (kʌm), *blood* (blʌd)
əː	as in *fern* (fəːn), *bird* (bəːd), *work* (wəːk)
ə	as in *admit* (ədˈmit), *famous* (ˈfeiməs), *bitter* (ˈbitə)

Diphthongs

ei	as in *make* (meik), *weigh* (wei), *say* (sei)
ou	as in *go* (gou), *road* (roud), *roll* (roul)
ai	as in *time* (taim), *cried* (kraid), *buy* (bai)
au	as in *loud* (laud), *cow* (kau), *flower* (flauə)
ɔi	as in *boy* (bɔi), *coin* (kɔin)
iə	as in *ear* (iə), *here* (hiə), *fierce* (fiəs)
ɛə	as in *air* (ɛə), *bear* (bɛə), *spare* (spɛə)
ɔə	as in *oar* (ɔə), *pore* (pɔə), *course* (kɔəs) (*N.B.* Many speakers of R.P. do not use this sound at all, but instead use the pure vowel ɔː.)
uə	as in *sure* (ʃuə), *poor* (puə), *curious* (ˈkjuəriəs), *influence* (ˈinfluəns) (*N.B.* Some people say ʃɔə, pɔə, ˈkjɔəriəs; and some say ˈinfluːəns.)

Semi-Vowels

| w | as in *wait* (weit), *quite* (kwait), *one* (wʌn) |
| j | as in *yes* (jes), *onion* (ˈʌnjən), *pew* (pjuː) |

Consonants

p	as in *peel* (piːl), *spark* (spɑːk)
b	as in *bee* (biː), *robin* (ˈrɔbin), *club* (klʌb)
t	as in *took* (tuk), *step* (step), *missed* (mist)
d	as in *deed* (diːd)
k	as in *come* (kʌm), *sky* (skai)
g	as in *geese* (giːs), *egg* (eg)
tʃ	as in *church* (tʃəːtʃ), *picture* (ˈpiktʃə)
dʒ	as in *judge* (dʒʌdʒ), *soldier* (ˈsouldʒə)
m	as in *make* (meik), *comfort* (ˈkʌmfət)
n	as in *not* (nɔt), *any* (ˈeni)
ŋ	as in *sang* (sæŋ), *ink* (iŋk), *younger* (ˈjʌŋgə)
l	as in *leak* (liːk), *look* (luk), *old* (ould)
f	as in *far* (fɑː), *rough* (rʌf)

v	as in *voice* (vɔis), *nephew* (ˈnevjuː)
θ	as in *thin* (θin), *north* (nɔːθ)
ð	as in *this* (ðis), *father* (ˈfɑːðə)
s	as in *sit* (sit), *place* (pleis)
z	as in *zoo* (zuː), *trees* (triːz), *scissors* (ˈsizəz)
ʃ	as in *shoe* (ʃuː), *special* (speʃl), *nation* (neiʃn)
ʒ	as in *pleasure* (ˈpleʒə), *occasion* (əˈkeiʒn)
r	as in *red* (red), *very* (ˈveri), *prove* (pruːv)
h	as in *hit* (hit), *behind* (biˈhaind)

The stress-sign ˈ is placed before the stressed syllable; for example the word *behind* is transcribed as biˈhaind. A lowered stress-sign, ˌ, is used to indicate secondary stress, that is, a degree of stress intermediate between strong and weak; for example, the word *administration*, as spoken in isolation, would be transcribed ədˌminisˈtreiʃn. The symbol ː indicates that the preceding sound is long. Further symbols will be introduced as required.

This system of transcription has some shortcomings. It is not very economical of symbols: it would be easy, for example, to dispense with ɛ, æ and ɔ, replacing them by e, a and o. Moreover, the system rather suggests by its form that the sounds i and iː are differentiated only by length, and similarly with u and uː, ɔ and ɔː; in fact this is not so: i differs from iː in quality as well as in length, and the same is true for the other pairs. You can test this very easily by making the sound u (as for example in *put*) and prolonging it: you will find that the result is not uː. However, despite these disadvantages, the system is a convenient one to use, because it is well-known and widely used for the teaching of English abroad, and is the system used by Daniel Jones in his *Pronouncing Dictionary* and other works.

It must also be realised that, while this system is adequate for our purposes, it does not represent all the different speech-sounds used by a speaker of R.P. You may have noticed this while reading through the examples: you may have noticed, perhaps, that in my three examples of the sound uː (*do*, *rule*, and *cube*) three different variants of the uː-sound are used; that the l in *leak* is different from that in *old*; that the p in *peel* differs slightly from that in *spark*; and so on. Unless you are a northerner, you can make a very quick test on the last example: hold the palm of your hand about an inch in front of your mouth, and pronounce aloud and vigorously first the word *park* and then the word *spark*; in *park*, the p is followed by a strong expulsion of breath, which can be felt on the hand; in *spark*, this puff of breath is absent or much reduced. This difference can also be heard, if you listen carefully. We can say that the p of *park* is aspirated, while that of *spark* is unaspirated or only weakly aspirated, and if we wished we could show this difference by transcribing the first by [pʰ] and the second by [p]; this however is unnecessary for all normal purposes, because the difference between the two is not significant linguistically: the meaning of an utterance in English can never be altered by replacing one of these sounds by the other (which is why a native speaker does not usually notice the difference between them). There are in fact several variants of the p-sound in R.P., but the variant used on any occasion is determined automatically by the phonetic context: one type is used before long vowels, another before short vowels, another before t, another after s, and so on: in other words, these variants of the p-sound in English have *complementary distribution*. Such a group of similar speech-sounds with complementary distribution is called a *phoneme*, and the system of transcription I have given above in fact has one symbol (or in some cases one digraph) for each phoneme of R.P.: it is a *phonemic transcription* or a *broad transcription*. Notice that the different variants of a phoneme (the different *allophones*) are heard in the speech of a single speaker: this is quite a different thing from the way in which speakers of different dialects vary from one another.

It is easy to see that changes in pronunciation can be of several different kinds. First, a change may consist simply in the replacement (in a given word) of one phoneme by another: for example, a northern speaker who pronounces *Monday* as ˈmʌndei may change his pronunciation to ˈmʌndi, under the influence of R.P. or of southern speech; he has simply put his i-phoneme into the word in place of his ei-phoneme. Secondly, a phoneme may disappear from a word completely, or may disappear regularly from certain positions; a historical example of the latter in English is provided by all such words as *knight*

and *knee*, which until early Modern English times were pronounced with an initial kn-, but in Present-day English are
pronounced with initial n-, the k having been lost during the
seventeenth century. Thirdly, a phoneme (or members of it)
can change in quality: we have already seen how M.E. i: developed into P.E. ai, and how the u-sound of early Modern English
changed into P.E. ʌ. Fourthly, there may be changes in the
whole phonemic structure of a language: entirely new phonemes may appear, others disappear. For example, in P.E. we
have the two phonemes θ and ð, but in Old English these were
merely allophones of a single phoneme: which of them was used
in a given word depended solely on the phonetic context, so
that they could never be used to distinguish between two words.
To-day, however, they form two phonemes, as you will see if
you consider the two words *thigh* (θai) and *thy* (ðai), which are
distinguished solely by the contrast between θ and ð. Again,
after early Modern English u had become ʌ, a new u-phoneme
arose, mainly by the shortening of u: in certain words, such as
good and *cook*; so P.E. has two phonemes where early Modern
English had only one, though in some English dialects there is
in fact no u/ʌ distinction: but the existence of two phonemes in
R.P. is shown by such pairs as *put* (put) and *putt* (pʌt). Fifthly,
there can be prosodic changes, that is changes in stress and
intonation; in the present century, for example, a number of
two-syllable words have had the stress moved from the second
syllable to the first (*e.g.*, the nouns *adult* and *ally*); and any
careful reader of Shakespeare will have realised that he frequently stresses words in a way that is strange to us (*revénue,
Júly*, the verb *to envý*, etc.).

Most of the changes discussed in this chapter will be of the
second and third types, but there will also be some examples of
the first and fifth. The time-scale is too short for one to feel
confident about any changes of the fourth type. I shall concentrate on R.P. and on educated south-eastern speech, which
(as I suggested in the last chapter) is now coming to be included in the concept of R.P.

When I give examples of pronunciations heard from B.B.C.
announcers, I always mean announcers who speak R.P. or a
form of educated south-eastern English very close to R.P.; none

of the quotations, in other words, are taken from announcers
with marked regional characteristics in their speech (such as
can be heard, for example, from the Manchester studio). I refer
so often to B.B.C. announcers simply as a matter of convenience,
since they are often heard pronouncing words which are otherwise not commonly spoken; moreover, of course, one can transcribe their remarks without difficulty, and without putting them
off their stroke. However, I never give examples which I have
heard only from B.B.C. announcers; and my examples in general are to be taken as merely illustrative, as small samples of
the kind of thing that can be heard quite commonly by anybody
who listens for it.

I shall deal first with the vowels, then with the consonants
(including semi-vowels), and then with a number of miscellaneous points (assimilation, weak forms, dialect-mixing, changes of
stress, spelling-pronunciations, "Continental" pronunciations).
For clarity, I shall break the material down into sections.

1. THE VOWELS

A. GENERAL

We can define vowels in several different ways, according to the
level of the language which we are considering: it is possible,
for example, to divide the English phonemes into two groups,
closely corresponding to the traditional vowels and consonants,
solely on the basis of their distribution within words; at a different level, vowels could be defined as those phonemes which
are preceded by a particular form of the indefinite article (ən
instead of ə). For our purposes, it will be sufficient to consider
the characteristics of vowels purely at the phonetic level; at this
level, we can say that a vowel is a voiced sound (that is, one
accompanied by the vibration of the vocal cords) in which
there is a free flow of air out of the mouth, without any audible
friction or any obstruction of the mouth-cavity.

Vowels differ from one another in various ways. They can
differ in length: on the average, the English i-sound is shorter
than the English iː-sound; however, there is no pair of English
vowel-phonemes which is distinguished solely by length, since
there are always also differences of quality.

Differences in quality between vowels are mainly due to two things, the position of the lips (whether or not the lips are rounded, and if so how tightly), and the position of the tongue (which alters the shape of the resonance-chamber formed by the mouth-cavity). A little experimentation with your finger in your mouth, or with a small mirror, will show you that the tongue moves progressively backwards in the mouth as you speak the sequence of sounds iː, əː, uː; these are *front, central,* and *back* sounds respectively. With the sequence iː, i, e, æ, you will find that the tongue gets progressively lower in the mouth; according to the height of the tongue, we can describe vowels as *close, mid,* or *open* (with intermediate positions called *half-close* and *half-open*). It is convenient to describe a vowel by the position of the highest point of the tongue, and this is often done by marking it by a dot on a *vowel-diagram*, which is a conventionalised cross-section of the mouth-cavity as seen from the left-hand side. Here is a vowel-diagram showing the tongue-positions of the English pure-vowel phonemes in R.P. (or at any

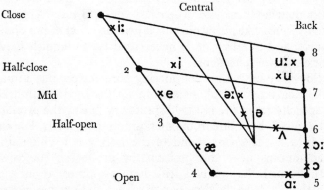

Vowel-diagram for the pure vowels of English (Received Pronunciation) after Daniel Jones (1932). The positions of the English vowels are shown by crosses. The positions of the cardinal vowels are shown by dots, and are numbered: 1. as *i* in French *si*; 2. as *é* in French *thé*; 3. as *è* in French *même*; 4. as *a* in French *la*; 5. as *a* in French *pas*; 6. as *o* in German *Sonne*; 7. as *o* in French *rose*; 8. as *u* in German *gut*.

rate the commonest allophones of them) according to Professor Daniel Jones in 1932; the diagram also shows the so-called *Cardinal Vowels* (numbered from 1 to 8), which are used as standard points of reference.

You can demonstrate to yourself the effect of *lip-rounding* on vowel-quality by making a prolonged iː-sound, and rounding your lips to the position for uː (being careful not to change your tongue-position meanwhile); the result will be a sound somewhat like the vowel of the French word *tu*. However, lip-rounding is not an independent variable in the formation of English vowels, since there is a direct correlation between lip-rounding and tongue-position: only the four backmost vowels have lip-rounding, and the degree of rounding becomes progressively tighter as the vowels become closer (so that ɔ has very open lip-rounding, and uː has tight lip-rounding).

In some languages, like French, the presence or absence of *nasalisation* is a distinctive feature of vowels (compare *mais* and *main*); in the nasalised vowel, the velum (the muscular back part of the roof of the mouth) is lowered so that air can flow out through the nasal cavity as well as through the mouth. English vowels are not normally nasalised; a vowel is occasionally somewhat nasalised when it is next to nasal consonants (*e.g.*, in words like *man*), but this is just the effect of the phonetic context, and nasalisation is never used to distinguish between different vowel-phonemes.

So far we have been considering pure vowels, but a number of the English vowel-phonemes are *diphthongs*. In a diphthong, the speech-organs are not held stationary during the production of the sound, but glide from one position to another. For example, in R.P. the vowel-sound of the word *boy* begins with the speech-organs near the position for producing the vowel ɔ (actually with the tongue a trifle higher); almost at once, however, they glide in the direction of i (though they may not move all the way there). It is the glide itself which constitutes the vowel, though the speech-organs may remain stationary for a short time in the initial position before the glide begins. A glide of this kind is not usually considered to be a diphthong unless it consists of only one syllable. A syllable can be defined as a peak of loudness: if a speaker's actual acoustic power-output is measured (say in microwatts) and plotted against time, it is found to contain small peaks of amplitude which correspond to what are traditionally called syllables. In normal English speech, the word *fie* (faɪ) contains only one syllable, while *fire* (faɪə) contains two (though some people smooth it down to one); *poor* (puə) has only one syllable, while *fewer* (ˈfjuːə) has two. We therefore consider aɪ and uə to be diphthongs, but uːə to be a sequence of two pure vowels. At the phonemic level, there is disagreement among linguists about the status of the English diphthongs: some treat them as single phonemes (as I am doing), some treat them as sequences of two phonemes (a vowel and a semi-vowel), and some again divide them into groups and treat some one way, some the other.

B. CHANGES OF VOWEL-QUALITY

(a) Isolative Changes

These are changes that take place irrespective of the phonetic position occupied by the phoneme.

Change in ʌ

This seems a clear case of a phoneme that has changed somewhat in quality in the present century, and it was commented on by Miss Ida Ward some years ago. The ʌ-sound (the one heard in *cup, butter,* etc.) is described by Daniel Jones in his *Outline of English Phonetics* as a half-open and rather retracted sound; the part of the tongue which is highest, he says, is the fore part of the back, and he shows it on his vowel-diagram as being decidedly more retracted than the central sounds ə and əː. To-day, the ʌ-sound seems to be made considerably further forward and lower than this, at any rate by the younger generation; it has moved in the direction of the French a-sound in words like *chat* and *toit*, though in most people's speech it has not got as far as that, but is an open central sound.

Change in ɔː

This is the vowel heard in *law, short,* etc. It is a retracted and rather open sound; in 1932 Jones described the height of the tongue as being between half-open and open, that is, between the vowel of German *Sonne* and that of French *pas*. It seems to me that in recent years it has come to be made with the jaw less open and the tongue slightly higher than formerly: that is, it has moved further away from the position of English ɔ (as in *hot*, etc.) and come nearer to the half-open position (that of the vowel of *Sonne*): indeed, in the speech of many people, it has very nearly reached half-open. The older, opener version of the vowel is still heard, and is characteristic of old-fashioned upper-class speech.

Change in ai

In much educated speech to-day, the diphthong ai (as in the word *time*) begins in a more retracted position than formerly; as described by Jones, ai begins from a low front position, not far from that of the a of French *patte*: but many people to-day begin it much nearer the position of English ɑː (as in *father*), and their diphthong could well be transcribed as [ɑi]. Miss Ida Ward calls this a "Cockney" pronunciation, but it is now quite common in educated south-eastern speech. I am not sure whether this pronunciation is spreading, or whether we merely have here an example of change of acceptance.

Centering of short vowels

There is a tendency (also pointed out by Miss Ida Ward) for all short vowels to be made nearer the centre of the mouth, that is, to move towards ə, especially in rapid familiar speech. This is particularly noticeable in certain common words, for example *yes* and *good*, in which the e and u often move very close to ə in position, and the u tends to lose its lip-rounding. This centripetal tendency is shared by the starting-position of the diphthong ou (as in *boat*, *hoe*, etc.), which for many speakers could now quite well be represented as [əu].

(b) Combinative Changes

These are changes that take place only in certain phonetic contexts. In a diachronic study, however, there is not always a sharp boundary between isolative and combinative changes, since a change often begins in one kind of phonetic context and then gradually spreads to others, until ultimately it has affected all members of the phoneme.

Change of ɔː *to* ɔ *before* f, s, *and* θ

It might be thought that an example of a combinative change in Present-day English was the change of ɔː to ɔ in a group of words where it precedes the voiceless fricatives f, s, and θ. Examples of such words are *cross* (krɔːs, krɔs), *toss* (tɔːs, tɔs), *soft* (sɔːft, sɔft), *off* (ɔːf, ɔf), *often* (ˈɔːfən, ˈɔfən), *cloth* (klɔːθ, klɔθ), and similarly *broth, lost, frost,* and many others. However, you will notice that not all words in which stressed ɔː is followed by f, s, or θ are undergoing this change: we still pronounce *horse, force, fourth,* and *sauce* as hɔːs, fɔːs, fɔːθ, and sɔːs. Why is this? The fact is, this change of ɔː to ɔ is not a phonetic change going on at the present time: a change took place almost two centuries ago in certain styles of speech, and two kinds of form, one with a long vowel and one with a short, have existed side by side in the language ever since; what is happening now is that one style is becoming fashionable at the expense of the other. It is, as a matter of fact, the original form (or rather its descendant) that is now becoming predominant, and the innovation that is dying out, not *vice versa*. All the words in question had a short o in Middle English; this became lengthened before s, f, and θ in the late seventeenth century in the speech of some groups, and the lengthened forms became fashionable in the eighteenth century. Now, however, they are becoming unfashionable again, and indeed are dying out. This is the kind of thing that happens when social groups go up or down in the world, and it is possible that the spread of the ɔ-forms in the present century is the result of social changes, especially the rise of democracy.

Change of ju: *to* u:

A change that *is* going on at the present time is that of ju: to u: in certain positions. This is a continuation of something that has been going on since the seventeenth century. In early Modern English there was a diphthong iu, derived from various Middle English sounds (mainly the diphthongs eu and iu and the high front rounded vowel y:), which in the seventeenth century became juː. Since that time, this juː has changed to uː in words where it is preceded by tʃ, dʒ, or r, or by consonant-plus-l; examples of this are *chew* (tʃuː), *June* (dʒuːn), *rule* (ruːl), and *blue* (bluː). In most positions, however, the juː has been retained, as in *music* (ˈmjuːzik), *pew* (pjuː), *due* (djuː), *huge* (hjuːdʒ), and so on. There is an intermediate group where both forms are heard, and it is in this group that the process of change is under way. Both forms are heard after s, as in *suit* (sjuːt, suːt); after θ, as in *enthusiasm* (inˈθjuːziæzm, inˈθuːziæzm); after z, as in *resume* (riˈzjuːm, riˈzuːm); after initial l, as in *lute* (ljuːt, luːt); and after medial l when it is preceded by an unstressed vowel, as in *absolute* (ˈæbsəljuːt, ˈæbsəluːt). In words where both forms are heard, the forms with uː are gaining ground at the expense of those with juː. The change is most advanced after l; for example, uː is almost universal in *lunatic*, and very common in *lunar*. After s, the juː is still quite common, but uː is now respectable: *suit* is frequently pronounced suːt, and from B.B.C. announcers I have heard *assume* and *consume* as əˈsuːm and kənˈsuːm. After z the change is less marked, and until quite recently the uː forms sounded dialectal; however, they are now beginning to appear in educated speech, and B.B.C. announcers sometimes use such pronunciations as riˈzuːm (*resume*). As in many things, the process has gone farther in American English than in British, and many British juː-pronunciations sound affected to American ears.

You should notice, by the way, that not all uː-sounds in P.E. are descended from iu; some are descended from Middle English long oː, as in *food*, *cool*, and *soon*; in such words there is no alternation between uː and juː. The different origin of the uː, it will be seen, is still reflected in the spelling: compare *cute* and *coot*, *beauty* and *boot*, *few* and *food*.

Diphthongisation of iː *and* uː

As described by Jones, both uː and iː are pure vowels; in other words, the speech-organs do not move appreciably while the sounds are being made. However, these sounds are now made into diphthongs by many speakers, especially in word-final position (as in *who* and *see*). Some speakers make them into diphthongs in other positions too, but the change is most marked and most frequent in word-final position, which is why I am dealing with it under Combinative Changes. It seems very likely, however, that the change will gradually spread to all positions.

In the case of uː, the diphthong used by educated speakers begins in about the position of u, and glides to the uː-position as described by Jones. If we wished to distinguish it from the pure uː, we could transcribe it as [ʊu]. When uː is a pure vowel, it has closer lip-rounding and a narrower jaw-opening than u, and people who use the [ʊu] variant usually tighten their lip-rounding and narrow their jaw-opening in the course of the diphthong. If you are doubtful whether you make a pure vowel or a diphthong, stand in front of a mirror and say uːuːuːuː...; if you use a diphthong, you will almost certainly see your lips tightening and relaxing and your lower jaw moving up and down slightly. In some people's speech, the diphthong has developed even further, and begins somewhere near ə; we can transcribe this variant as [əu]; it is heard from some educated people, especially younger ones, but still sounds decidedly sub-standard to most speakers of R.P.

Similarly, iː is often made into a diphthong beginning near the position of i and moving up to the position that iː has when it is a pure vowel; this variant can be transcribed as [ɪi]. Once again, there is a more "advanced" form of the diphthong, which can be transcribed as [əi], which is heard from some educated people but must still be considered sub-standard.

All these diphthongs are *falling* ones: that is, they have their greatest sonority and stress at the beginning, and these die away in the course of the diphthong.

Smoothing of diphthongs

While new diphthongs are thus being formed, there is perhaps a tendency for some of the existing diphthongs to be smoothed out, that is, for the glide to become shorter, so that they are more like pure vowels. This process of monophthong-isation is especially seen in ei (the sound of *say*, *plain*, etc.); the glide in this sound is now very slight, and in some people's speech it is not far removed from a long pure vowel of the eː type. The diphthongs ai and au are subject to a smoothing

process when they are followed by ə, as in *tower* (ˈtauə) and *fire*
(ˈfaiə): these groups both tend to be smoothed down to a diphthong of the [aə] type, so that some people say [faə] and [taə].
Some people smooth them even further to a pure vowel, [aː] or
[ɑː], and say [faː] and [taː] (or [fɑː] and [tɑː], with permutations).
This smoothing of aiə and auə is commoner in R.P. proper than
in educated regional speech.

Final iː *for* i

When i comes at the end of a word, many people use an
allophone that is much closer than normal i, and sometimes
longer. With some speakers, the i is sufficiently long and close
to sound like their normal iː, and it seems justifiable to assert
that in such cases the i is in fact replaced by iː. This usage can
be heard in the speech of many educated people from the south-
east, who tend to pronounce *pretty* and *Derby* as ˈpritiː and
ˈdɑːbiː, instead of the usual ˈpriti and ˈdɑːbi. This is not heard,
however, from public-school speakers, that is from speakers of
R.P. in the narrower (or older) sense: they, on the contrary, tend
to make final i into an opener sound, moving it in the direction
of e; indeed, to many non-standard speakers, the public-school
man's pronunciation of *pretty* often sounds as though it were
ˈprite, especially at the end of a phrase. The use of final iː for i
is heard, however, in some American speech, and also in Australian and New Zealand speech: it is often heard, for example,
in the Australian pronunciation (or at any rate one Australian
pronunciation) of *Sydney*. When an inflexional ending is added
to a word with one of these final iː sounds, the iː is usually
retained; I have often been struck by the pronunciation by
B.B.C. announcers of such words as *authorities*, with a final -iːz.

Englishmen who use this final iː are often also ones who
diphthongise their iː-sounds, and this final iː shares in the diphthongisation— which is evidence that this sound should indeed
be considered to belong to the iː-phoneme. By such people,
pretty comes to sound something like [ˈpritɩ] or [ˈpritəi]. Variants of this final diphthong can be heard in different parts of
the country from children shouting "Mummy!".

The use of iː for final i, however, seems not to be a change
that has occurred in our own time, but rather another example

of a change in acceptance, for there is evidence of the iː-pro-
nunciation from earlier periods.

Occasionally in educated speech i is replaced by iː in other
positions. Examples heard from B.B.C. announcers include
between as biːˈtwiːn (instead of biˈtwiːn) and *eleven* as iːˈlevn
(instead of iˈlevn). It is possible, however, that these are merely
over-careful pronunciations.

Change in final iə

Another change found especially in word-final position is
the replacement of the diphthong iə, which is one syllable, by
the sequence of i followed by ə, which is two; we can transcribe
this as i-ə. For example, I have heard B.B.C. announcers pronounce *Rhodesia* as rouˈdiːsi-ə, and from other educated speakers
I have heard *nausea* as ˈnɔːsi-ə, and *dubious* as ˈdjuːbi-əs (usually
it is ˈdjuːbiəs or ˈdjuːbjəs). In this last example, the i-ə is not
word-final, but it is (like the other examples) unstressed. I cannot recall having heard i-ə for iə in final stressed position in
educated speech, but it may be possible (in words like *cavalier*
and *chandelier*, for example). You can also hear i-ə for iə in
stressed medial position and in monosyllables, but not, I think,
in educated speech: pronunciations like ˈhi-ə and ˈri-əli for *here*
and *really* are probably sub-standard.

There is perhaps a similar (but less marked) tendency for
the diphthong uə to be replaced by the sequence u-ə; I think
I have noticed this in such words as *influence* and *arduous*: but it
is possible that the sequence here was uːə rather than u-ə.

These changes in iə and uə are perhaps spelling-pronunciations.

The influence of "dark l"

A sound which frequently influences a preceding vowel is
the English l. This is a *lateral* consonant: to produce it, you
press the tip of the tongue against the teeth-ridge, thus blocking
the centre of the mouth-passage, but let air escape down one
side. The main body of the tongue can occupy various positions in the mouth, according to the neighbouring sounds, so
that there are numerous allophones of the English l-phoneme.
These fall into two main groups, usually called "clear l" and
"dark l" (or, more portentously, "l with velar co-articulation").

In clear l, the front of the tongue is raised; in dark l, the back of the tongue is raised, so that the shape of the resonance-chamber formed by the mouth-cavity is approximately as for the sound u; indeed, foreigners often mistake dark l for some kind of u-sound. In R.P., dark l occurs only before consonants (except j) and before a pause; clear l occurs in all other positions. Thus clear l occurs in *holly, leap, molest,* and *look;* dark l occurs in *old, health,* and *Alps,* and in *feel* and *double* when these words are pronounced in isolation.

Dark l often influences the preceding vowel, and many English vowel-phonemes have special allophones that occur only in this position; in many people's speech, for example, there are special variants of uː and of ou which occur only before dark l (listen to your own speech and see if this is true of you). Sometimes the influence is even more powerful, and there is an actual change of phoneme. For example, in south-eastern speech the group ɔlv is often replaced by oulv, as in *revolve, solve, dissolve,* etc., and this variant is perhaps becoming commoner in educated speech. This is probably another example of a change of style, the differentiation into two pronunciations having taken place a good time ago; if so, it is another example of a lower-middle-class or lower-class pronunciation permeating upwards into the professional classes as a result of the social changes of our age. There is a somewhat similar alternation of pronunciation in words with ɔlt or ɔːlt, such as *salt, falter, halt,* etc., but in this case both forms seem equally respectable socially; the ɔː forms are gaining ground at the expense of the ɔ forms.

In some dialects, and notably Cockney, dark l develops into a kind of u or ɔ, often forming a diphthong with the preceding vowel; so that *old* becomes ɔud, and *milk* miuk, and so on. There are slight signs that this tendency is beginning to affect educated speech; in familiar speech, even speakers of R.P. sometimes say ˈʃæu wiː for *shall we?*; I have heard B.B.C. announcers pronounce *Wales* as ˈwæuz; and on the Third Programme I have heard a distinguished elder scientist (apparently a speaker of R.P.) use forms like ðəmˈseuvz for *themselves.*

The spread of ə in unstressed syllables

In a considerable number of English words there are alternative forms of vowels in unstressed syllables; the commonest alternations are between ə and some other short vowel. To some extent the choice between an ə-form and a form with another vowel depends on the speed and care with which the speaker is talking, but I do think that at the same time there is a tendency for the ə-forms to gain ground.

Very common are alternations between i and ə; thus *system* can be pronounced ˈsistim or ˈsistəm, *exact* can be igˈzækt, or əgˈzækt, *ability* can be əˈbiliti or əˈbiləti; and similarly with *corporate, become, remain, horrible, waitress, kitchen,* and many others. Forms which I have heard from B.B.C. announcers, and which have struck me as unusual, are *women* (ˈwimən), *useless* (ˈjuːsləs), and *engine* (ˈendʒən).

There are also alternations with other vowels, and some of these are probably new in R.P. The following are all examples heard from B.B.C. announcers: ə replacing e: *September* (səpˈtembə), the verb *implement* (ˈimpləmənt), perhaps by analogy with the noun *implement*; ə replacing æ: *handicapped* (ˈhændikəpt), *diplomat* (ˈdipləmət), *enthusiast* (inˈθuːziəst); ə replacing ɔ: *boycotted* (ˈbɔikətid), *corridor* (ˈkɔridə); ə replacing ʌ: *sawdust* (ˈsɔːdəst), *income* (ˈinkəm); ə replacing ei or i: *candidate* (ˈkændidət).

Once again, American and Australian speech have gone further than British, and use ə in many words where it would hardly be possible in R.P.: for example in the noun *minute* and *damage* (in R.P. ˈminit and ˈdæmidʒ); and in the plural ending *-es* and the past-tense ending *-ed* in words like *boxes* and *ended* (where R.P. uses -iz and -id). But it does look as though the use of ə is spreading more widely in British speech.

C. CHANGES OF VOWEL-LENGTH

English vowels vary in length according to the phonetic context—the degree of stress they bear, whether they are followed by a voiced or by a voiceless consonant, the number of unstressed syllables before and after them, and so on. However, given an identical phonetic context, some of the vowels are longer than others, and there is quite a considerable range of variation; iː for example is appreciably longer than ɑː, and ɑː is a good deal longer than e, which is itself longer than ə. It is convenient, however, to divide the vowels into two groups, the long and the short; the vowels usually considered short are i, e, æ, ʌ, ɔ, u, and ə; the remaining pure vowels and the diphthongs are usually regarded as long.

In our time, however, there are changes going on in vowel-length. In particular, there is a strong tendency for the so-called short vowels to be lengthened. This inevitably happens in any case when there are intonation-changes inside the syllable which require a certain length of vowel to manifest themselves, so that the speaker drags the length of the vowel out; this can be heard very easily when a fall-rise intonation is used, that is when the pitch of the voice first falls then rises again within one syllable, as when "Ye-es" is said in a tone of lingering doubt and hesitation; here the normally short vowel e becomes decidedly long. The important thing, however, is that the lengthening of short vowels is not confined to such positions, but is heard sporadically in any position in many words, which vary from speaker to speaker. A lengthened i is often heard in *big, his,* and *is,* a lengthened u in *good,* a lengthened ʌ in *come;* all these words are monosyllables ending in a voiced consonants and it is in fact in such words that the lengthening is most frequent. The short vowels which are lengthened most frequently are e and æ. The lengthening of e is often heard in *yes, bed, men,* and *said,* among others. Even commoner is the lengthening of æ, which is often heard in *man, bag, bad, jam,* and so on; the words which have the lengthened vowel vary from speaker to speaker, but the lengthening is particularly common in London speech. Jones remarks that in the south of England a fully long æ is generally used in the adjectives ending in *-ad (bad, sad,* etc.), but not in the nouns ending in *-ad (lad, pad,* etc.). In my own speech, all the adjectives in *-ad* have a long vowel; of the nouns, *lad* has a long vowel, but *cad, fad, dad,* and *pad* have short ones.

This sporadic lengthening of short vowels in words which vary somewhat from speaker to speaker looks very much like the early stage of a large-scale change. Jones remarked some years ago that the tendency to lengthen short vowels was on the increase, and suggested that perhaps a new development of the language was beginning, whereby the present distinctions between vowels based on both quality and length will give way to a distinction based on quality only. As in many other things, American English has developed further in this direction than British.

Is there any pattern to be seen in all these various vowel-changes? One would expect there to be, because a language is a system of interrelated parts, and one part cannot change without affecting the others. However, we must not expect too much: for one thing, we are working with a very short time-scale; and for another, the process of dialect-mixing which is going on may mean that some of the changes I have described really belong to different styles of speech, are parts of somewhat different systems. However, we can see one or two consistent trends. The short vowels all seem to be becoming slightly more central in position, and also have a tendency to be lengthened. The two long close vowels, iː at the front and uː at the back, are both being diphthongised; here we have an interesting parallel with what happened in the great vowel-shift which took place between Middle English and Modern English, in which Middle English iː and uː became diphthongs and ulti-mately developed into Present-day English ai and au. The point of drawing this parallel is that in the great vowel-shift this diphthongisation was just one part of a complete change of pattern in the long vowels; is anything like this happening to-day? As iː and uː become diphthongs, are other phonemes moving up to fill the places left vacant? I can see no sign of this, though the change in ɔː, which has been getting closer, would fit in well with such a pattern of change. But it is really too early to tell.

2. THE CONSONANTS

A. GENERAL

At the phonetic level, we can define a *consonant* negatively from the definition we have already given of a vowel: all speech-sounds which are not vowels are consonants.

The English consonants fall into three main groups. First

there are the *stops*: in such sounds, the stream of air from the
lungs is blocked by closure of the air-passage at some point;
pressure is built up behind the stoppage, and then this pressure
is suddenly released by the opening of the closure. The release
of the stop may be very rapid, as in p, t, and k, in which case
the stop is called a *plosive*; or it may be relatively slow, as in tʃ,
in which case the stop is called an *affricate*.

Secondly, there are the *fricatives*. In these, there is a continuous flow of air through the mouth, but the air-passage is
narrowed at some point so that audible friction is produced.
The constriction may be in many different places: between the
lower lip and the upper teeth, as in f, between the tip of the
tongue and the teeth, as in θ, and so on. The acoustic effect is
also influenced by the shape of the passage provided: in s and z
for example, there is a very narrow channel down the middle
of the tongue, and this gives a very different sound from r,
which is articulated in about the same place (blade of tongue
against teeth-ridge) but without the narrow channel. It is convenient to include h among the fricatives, the audible friction
in this case occurring in the glottis.

Thirdly, there are the *resonants* or *sonorants* (terms which
include the vowels as well). In the resonant consonants, there
is a flow of air through resonant cavities, but there is nevertheless some kind of obstruction which distinguishes them from the
vowels. In the English *lateral* resonant, l, the centre of the
mouth-passage is blocked by the tongue, and the air is allowed
to pass down one side, or both. In the English *nasal* resonants,
m, n, and ŋ, the mouth-passage is completely closed at some
point, but the velum is lowered and the air allowed to flow out
freely through the nose. The three nasals differ from one another in the point where the closure is made (with the lips,
with the tip of the tongue against the teeth-ridge, with the
back of the tongue against the soft palate). Many people be-
lieve that all English syllables contain a vowel, but in fact the
nasals and laterals often form the nucleus of a syllable, as in
words like *little* (ˈlitl), *button* (ˈbʌtn), and *rhythm* (ˈriðm), all of
which are disyllabic. Under the resonants we can also include
the two English *semi-vowels*, j and w, which it is convenient to
treat with the consonants; these are non-syllabic glides, j start-

ing at about the position of i, and w at about the position of u; the direction of the glide depends entirely on the vowel that follows, since the semi-vowel consists of a glide *to* the following vowel.

To describe a consonant, we have to specify its mode of articulation (plosive, fricative, lateral, nasal, etc.), the articulating organ (lower lip, tip of tongue, blade of tongue, etc.), and the place of articulation (upper lip, teeth, teeth-ridge, palate, etc.). In addition, we have to say whether or not it is *voiced*. A voiced sound is one accompanied by a particular kind of vibration of the vocal cords (a different kind of vibration is heard for example in whispered speech). A speech-sound unaccompanied by any vibration of the vocal cords is said to be *voiceless* or *breathed*. Any speech-sound can be produced with or without voice, and most languages have numbers of pairs of similar consonants, with one member of the pair voiced and the other breathed. There are eight such pairs in English: t and d, p and b, k and g, s and z, ʃ and ʒ, tʃ and dʒ, f and v, and θ and ð. The remaining consonants are normally voiced, except for h, which is normally voiceless: but there is a voiced allophone of h, and voiceless allophones of the others, which are heard in particular phonetic contexts. A good test to see whether a sound is voiced or not is to stop up your ears with your hands and speak the sound aloud (being careful not to add a vowel to it); if it is voiced, you will hear the vibration in your head. Try it out by stopping up your ears, and pronouncing alternately a long sustained s and a long sustained z, thus s...z...s...z... etc.; the difference will be immediately apparent. You can also feel the vibration of the vocal cords by resting your fingers on the Adam's apple.

B. THE WEAKENING AND LOSS OF CONSONANTS

In some positions consonants are tending to be articulated weakly, and sometimes disappear altogether. The weakening is especially noticeable in word-final position, but also occurs in some other positions.

Final alveolars

The final consonants that especially show signs of weakening to-day are the alveolars, that is, those articulated on the teeth-ridge (the convex part of the roof of the mouth immediately behind the top teeth). Those that are particulary affected are the alveolar stops t and d, and the alveolar nasal n. For example, in rapid familiar speech, the final alveolars in the following phrases are weakly articulated, and sometimes disappear altogether: *fiftee(n) men; wha(t)'s the matter?; no(t) bad; ol(d) man*. A t especially tends to disappear between s and a following consonant, as in *half pas(t) five* and similar expressions of time.

Loss of plosives

Besides t and d, the other English plosives p, b, k, and g also show signs of disappearing in some positions. From the description given earlier of the way a stop is made, you will see that a plosive has three main phases: first a closure is formed, then the closure is held while pressure is built up behind it (this phase being a completely silent one), and finally the stop is released by a rapid opening of the closure. In some positions, however, the final stage is omitted completely: there is no release of the stop. One position where this happens is before another stop: in the word *knocked*, which is pronounced nɔkt, we do not release the closure of the k before going on to the t; we make the closure for k, then move to the closure for t, and only then do we release; and similarly with other pairs of stops, as in *begged, apt, ink-pot, bedtime*, and *egg-cup*. In such cases there is a possibility that the first of the plosives may disappear altogether, and this in fact often happens in some words and phrases: thus *sit down* often becomes siˈdaun in rapid familiar speech, instead of sitˈdaun; *asked* is very frequently pronounced ɑːst, even in educated speech; and B.B.C. announcers often pronounce *East Coast* as iːsˈkoust. In two of these three examples, you will notice, the stops are preceded by s, which seems especially powerful in causing the disappearance of the first of two succeeding consonants—as indeed it has been in the past, witness words like *Christmas* (ˈkrisməs) and *castle* (ˈkɑːsl).

Simplification of double consonants

In Old English, the words *bannan* and *banan* were pro-

nounced differently: the first was spoken with a long or doubled n, the second with a single n, and this made them into
two distinct words. A similar distinction between single and
double consonants is found in modern Italian and modern
Swedish. During the Old English and Middle English periods,
however, the doubled consonants were gradually simplified to
single ones, first in final position, ultimately in all positions.
However, although we no longer have doubled consonants
within simple words, new long or doubled consonants have
arisen in the language by the formation of new compound
words and set phrases. In expressions like *book-case* and *a good
deal*, the first of the two identical stops is not released, but the
stop is held for longer than usual; it is thus possible to hear the
difference between *that ale* (ðæt'eil) and *that tale* (ðæt'teil), because of the longer pause in the middle of the latter. (There is
in fact another difference between them, since the latter expression has a more strongly aspirated stop: but it is the length
of the stop rather than the aspiration that is distinctive.) However, there is now a tendency for such double consonants to be
simplified to single ones, especially in phrases where no ambiguity is produced by the change. An example which is often
heard is *a good deal* pronounced as əgu'di:l; and it is not uncommon to hear *upside-down* as 'ʌpsai'daun, and *lamp-post* as
'læmpoust. The habit is not confined to stops: in familiar
speech, it is often heard in expressions like *prime-minister*, *Chris-
tian name* and *gas-stove*

Initial ps *and* pt

In the small group of words beginning with ps, this consonant cluster is now usually simplified to s. The number of words
involved is small, all being derived from the Greek (*pseudo*,
psyche, and their derivatives). Pronunciations like 'psju:dou and
'psaiki are now very rare (except jocularly), and sound very
old-fashioned. The same is true of initial pt, which occurs only
in derivatives of the Greek *ptero-* (*e.g.*, *pterodactyl*); the pronunciation 'pter- is now very rare, and has been replaced by 'ter-.
These two initial clusters, ps and pt, do not accord with normal
English ways of forming initial consonant clusters, in which
stops are usually followed only by liquids (r and l) or by semi-

vowels (j and w); this is no doubt the reason why these rather learned pronunciations have fallen out of use.

Initial hw

Some speakers pronounce words like *where* and *what* with an initial hw in place of the more normal w. The general tendency, however, is for hw to die out and be replaced by w; indeed, hw probably persists only because of the spelling, and of the belief in some schools that hw is a more refined pronunciation than w. Most people say wɛə and wɔt.

Loss of h

The h phoneme is often lost, too, in other positions, and may be on its way out from the language. It is commonly thought that to "drop one's aitches" is a mark of vulgarity; in fact, however, in rapid familiar speech the h disappears from many words even in the most highly educated and socially impeccable speakers, though they may not be conscious of it. But in educated speech h is only lost at the beginning of an unstressed syllable or word: so in rapid educated speech the sentence *he gave him his breakfast* might well be iˈgeivim izˈbrekfəst. Loss of h at the beginning of a stressed syllable, however, is not heard in R.P., and does sound "vulgar." Still, what is vulgar to-day is often accepted to-morrow, and I shouldn't like to stake too much money on the future of the h phoneme in English.

C. THE DEVOICING OF CONSONANTS

There is a tendency for final voiced consonants, especially stops, to become devoiced. It is as a matter of fact normal for English voiced consonants to be partly devoiced in initial and final position: in a word like *views* (vjuːz), voice does not begin on the initial v until it is well under way, and similarly voice dies out on the z before it has ended. In final position, however, this tendency to devoicing now seems to be on the increase, and sometimes the final voiced consonant is completely devoiced; this happens especially with the voiced stops, b, d, and g. If we wish to indicate this devoicing in our transcription, we can write [b̥], [d̥], and [g̊]. Such devoiced sounds are especially heard after long vowels and diphthongs, as in *feed* [fiːd̥], *rogue* [rouɡ̊], and so on. Now you might think that, when a voiced consonant was devoiced, it became identical with the similarly articulated voiceless consonant, that [d̥] for example was identical with [t]. In fact this is not so, because in English the voiceless consonants are pronounced with strong breath-force, and the voiced consonants with weak breath-force (as you can again test for yourself by putting your hand in front of your mouth and saying pɑː and bɑː); when the voiced consonants become devoiced, they are still produced with weak breath-force, and so sound different from the ordinary voiceless consonants. However, this devoicing does reduce the contrast between the pairs of sounds.

D. THE VOICING OF CONSONANTS

While final voiced consonants often lose their voice, there is an opposite tendency in medial positions, especially between vowels: intervocalic voiceless consonants sometimes become voiced. Or perhaps it would be more accurate to say that they are sometimes pronounced with weak breath-force, and so sound like the corresponding voiced consonant. This is especially common with t followed by an unstressed consonant, in words like *letter*, *better*, and *latter*, which are sometimes pronounced [ˈled̥ə], [ˈbed̥ə], and [ˈlæd̥ə]. This, no doubt is still stigmatised as "careless" or "vulgar" (or even as "American", which for some people seems to mean the same thing): but I have heard B.B.C. announcers produce *British* as [ˈbrid̥iʃ], and this may be a development of significance for the future.

E. INTRUSIVE CONSONANTS

While some consonants are weakening and even disappearing, there are other positions where new consonants are appearing. I don't mean by this that new consonant phonemes are arising, but that consonants are being inserted into words where previously they did not exist.

Intrusive stops

One example of this in Present-day English is the tendency

for the group -ns- to change into -nts-, at any rate in the south of England. To a northern ear, it often sounds as though the southerner says ˈfæntsi and ˈfentsiŋ, for *fancy* and *fencing*, instead of ˈfænsi and ˈfensiŋ. The sound n is produced with the tongue in the same position as for t, blocking the mouth-passage by pressure of the tip against the teeth-ridge: but in n the velum or soft palate is lowered so that air can pass freely out through the nose, and the vocal cords are made to vibrate to produce voice. The change-over from n to s in a word like *fancy* involves three things: (1) the velum is raised to close the air-passage to the nose; (2) the vocal cords stop vibrating, since s is a voiceless sound; and (3) the shape of the tongue is altered slightly so that it has a channel down the middle along which air can flow out of the mouth with a hissing sound. Now what often happens in southern speech when -ns- is articulated is that (1) and (2) are carried out slightly earlier than (3); the result is that for a short time there is no passage for air through the nose, and there is no voice, but the mouth-passage is still completely blocked by the pressure of the tongue against the teeth-ridge: in other words the vocal organs are in the position for articulating t. Then the tongue moves into the position for s, and the stop is released by the flow of air out of the mouth that constitutes the s. This change of ns to nts happens most often when the group is preceded by a stressed vowel and followed by an unstressed one, as in the two examples I gave above, but it also happens in monosyllables, like the word *once*, which is sometimes pronounced wʌnts.

There is a similar tendency in the south for intrusive p and k to arise, but this is less common. It happens especially when the following sound is s, t, or θ. The p occurs after m, as in *warmth*, which is sometimes pronounced wɔːmpθ; and the k after ŋ, as when *length* is pronounced leŋkθ. The mechanism by which these intrusive sounds are produced is similar to that for t.

This kind of thing is not new in English, for there are various words in which, at some period or other, a voiceless stop has been gained or lost after a nasal. The word *empty* is descended from Old English æmettig, later æmtig; in Middle English this becomes *emti* or *empti*, and to-day it is pronounced either ˈemti or empti. Sometimes the same kind of thing has happened with

voiced stops: in *bramble* a b has been gained, and in *thunder* a d;
but this is old history.

Intrusive r

Another consonant-sound that is appearing in new positions
in R.P. is r. In Present-day English there are many words which
have an r in their spelling which is not pronounced, like *cord*
(kɔːd), *barn* (bɑːn), and *firm* (fəːm); this is also true of words like
father and *here* when they occur before a pause or before a consonant, and are then pronounced ˈfɑːðə and hiə. In such words,
there was in fact an r in the pronunciation until quite recently;
it was not until the seventeenth century that it became weakened, and it was not lost until the eighteenth century. It was
only lost when it occurred before a consonant-sound or before a
pause, and was retained when it occurred before a vowel-sound,
as in *very* and *barricade*. The result of this is that there are many
words in P.E., like *father* and *here*, which have an r in their pronunciation when they occur immediately before a word beginning with a vowel, but not otherwise. For example, the word
father, spoken in isolation, is ˈfɑːðə; and the sentence *father knows*
is ˈfɑːðə ˈnouz: but *father and mother* is ˈfɑːðərən ˈmʌðə. The r
used in this last phrase is called *linking* r.

Intrusive r is an r which is inserted in this way at the end of
a word which gives no historical justification for it, that is, a
word which had no r at the end in the days when r was pronounced in all positions. A good example of this is the word
idea in phrases like *the idea of it*, which is usually pronounced
ði aiˈdiər əv it; the fact that this is an unhistorical pronunciation
is of course reflected in the spelling.

Intrusive r is an example of the effect of *analogy*, which is
a potent factor both in language-learning and in linguistic
change. Analogy is the process by which a speaker constructs
a linguistic form in accordance with some pattern which (con-
sciously or unconsciously) he has perceived in the part of the
language which he has so far learnt (nobody ever learns the
whole of a language). Thus a child learning his mother-tongue
learns pairs like bed/beds, toy/toys, doll/dolls, and so on, in
which z is the mark of the plural; he then learns the word *school*,
and quite correctly constructs the plural form *schools* (skuːlz)

without ever having heard it. Analogy, of course, also leads him to make mistakes, which have to be corrected, as when from *man* he forms a plural *mans*, or from the verb *go* a past tense *goed*. Analogy operates, therefore, by the speaker constructing a paradigm or pattern for part of the language, and then solving a problem or completing a proportion in accordance with it. In the case of intrusive r, the speaker has a paradigm of this kind:

father was	(ˈfaːðə wəz)	*father and mother*	(ˈfaːðər ən ˈmʌðə)
here was	(hiə wəz)	*here and there*	(hiər ən ðɛə)
beer was	(ˈbiə wəz)	*beer and spirits*	(ˈbiər ən ˈspirits)
idea was	(aiˈdiə wəz)	*idea and reality*	(?)

The speaker completes the proportion by pronouncing *idea and reality* as aiˈdiər ən riˈæliti, and we have an intrusive r. The analogy of *father*, *here*, *beer* (and many other similar words) has determined the treatment of *idea*.

Intrusive r is very common after ə, which is to be expected, since there are so many words in which linking r occurs after ə, thus providing the basis for the analogy. In this position, intrusive r is common in educated speech, and seems rapidly to be becoming universal: it is regularly used by B.B.C. announcers, for example, after words like *India* and *Ghana*. It is less common after other vowels, and was formerly considered substandard in such positions; however, this distinction now seems to be breaking down, and many speakers of R.P. are beginning to use intrusive r in phrases like *the law of the sea* (ðə ˈlɔːr əv ðə ˈsiː).

The glottal stop

This is perhaps a sound that is spreading more widely in educated speech. In the glottal stop the closure is produced in the glottis, by the drawing together of the vocal cords; the cords are then opened suddenly to release the stop. It is a sound heard in German, before vowels at the beginning of a word. It can be transcribed as [ʔ]. The glottal stop is heard in some sub-standard English dialects, and notably in Cockney, where it is used in place of t (as when *butter* is pronounced [ˈbʌʔə]), and sometimes in place of the other voiceless plosives (as when *knock* is pronounced [nɔʔ]). It is also heard in educated speech, but only before certain consonants, and only in place of t, never of any other voiceless plosive. Moreover, I think that in educated speech it is rare for the glottal stop actually to replace the t: what happens much more frequently is that a t-closure and a ʔ-closure are made simultaneously, so that it would be more accurate to speak of a glottalised t than of a glottal stop. In educated speech, the glottal stop or a glottalised t is perhaps heard most frequently before m and n, as in *batman* [ˈbætmən, ˈbæʔmən] and *button* [ˈbʌtn, ˈbʌʔn]; it is also quite common before r, j, and w, as in phrases like *not right*, *not yet*, *not one*. Before other consonants, for example in *little* [liʔl], and before vowels, as in *butter* [ˈbʌʔə], it is sub-standard; even a glottalised t is sub-standard in these positions.

F. SOME CONSEQUENCES OF THE CONSONANT-CHANGES

Most of the consonant-changes described in sections B, C, and D have the effect of reducing the contrasts between different consonants. As a consequence, other criteria for distinguishing certain pairs of words have probably become more important: if the final consonant of *fifteen* becomes obscured, or the contrast reduced between the final consonants of *seat* and *seed*, we shall probably look for other ways of establishing differences of meaning clearly. One such means that we use is stress: this is how we distinguish between *fifteen men* and *fifty men*; in rapid speech, the final n of fifteen has little value for the making of the distinction, since it is hardly heard; the contrast between i and iː is not decisive either, since many southerners pronounce *fifty* as ˈfiftiː; what is really decisive nowadays for distinguishing between the phrases is the stress-pattern, the first being ˈfifˈtiːn ˈmen and the second ˈfifti ˈmen. That it is the stress-pattern (and the accompanying intonation-pattern) that is crucial is shown by the frequent confusions caused by foreign speakers of English who get the stress wrong: it is very common for the non-native speaker to pronounce *fifteen men* as ˈfiftiːn ˈmen, and almost invariably the unwary native listener will hear it as *fifty men*.

Another indication that we use, and that is probably becoming more important, is the varying length of the vowel. This is a particularly important signal that we pick up when it is difficult to distinguish between a voiced and a voiceless final consonant. In general, English vowels (and especially the long vowels) are longer before voiced consonants than before voiceless ones: other things being equal, the i: in *seed* is longer than that in *seat*, and this remains true even when the voiced consonant becomes devoiced. We probably make use of this fact for distinguishing between pairs like *seat* and *seed*, especially at the end of a phrase, when the final consonants are hardly distinguishable. Of course, the context is often enough to tell us which of a pair is meant, but when we listen to speech we usually insure against misunderstanding by picking up more signals than the minimum necessary: language always has a good deal of redundancy, to give a margin of safety. If I am right in thinking that the differences of vowel-length in *seat* and *seed* have some significance for the distinction of meanings, then this might possibly be the first stage of an important change: if it were to develop further, vowel-length alone might take on phonemic significance, and some of our present vowel-phonemes break up into two phonemes each, one long and one short: but of course this is highly conjectural.

3. ASSIMILATION

Having now given some account of the general changes affecting the English vowels and consonants in our times, I shall go on to discuss various miscellaneous sources of pronunciation-changes, which affect only odd words or groups of words. The first of these is *assimilation*.

Assimilation is the process by which a sound is altered through the influence of a neighbouring sound; the sound which is influenced becomes phonetically more like the sound exerting the influence. A historical example of assimilation is seen in the word *scant*: this is derived from the Scandinavian *skammt*, but at an early period the m was changed to n through the influence of t: an alveolar stop caused a preceding bilabial nasal to change into an alveolar nasal. Another example is the common pronunciation of *width* as witθ, beside earlier widθ: here the voiced stop d has changed to the voiceless stop t under the influence of the following voiceless fricative θ. These are both examples of *regressive* assimilation, that is, one in which

the sound exerting the influence comes later in the word than
the one influenced. A historical example of *progressive* assimilation is seen in words like *watch* (wɔtʃ), where the rounded
vowel ɔ is the result of the influence of the preceding w; in
Shakespeare's day, *watch* rhymed with *match*. We can also count
as assimilation the cases where two sounds operate on one another and coalesce to form a third sound; a historical example
of this in English is the development of ʃ from an earlier sj, in
words like *condition* and *musician* and *sugar*.

It is not always easy to be sure what assimilations have
taken place in our own time, and which go back to earlier
periods, as the traditional spelling of a word may be ambiguous.
Thus *newspaper* is commonly pronounced ˈnjuːspeipə, whereas
news is always njuːz; here z has become s under the influence of
the following voiceless p, but this is not reflected in the spelling,
and it is difficult to know exactly when it arose. However, it is
likely that the following examples of assimilation (given by
Jones) are relatively recent: əˈmitst for *amidst*, beikŋ for *bacon*,
ˈhæpm for *happen*, ˈoupm for *open*, ˈtʃuldrən for *children*, and
ˈpruti for *pretty*; these are all occasional pronunciations heard
alongside the more traditional ones. You may find it amusing
to listen for more examples in the speech of those around you.

Assimilations often occur where the elements of compound
words meet; thus *football* is often ˈfupbɔːl, while *ninepence* is often
ˈnaimpəns, *tenpence* is ˈtempəns, and *sevenpence* is ˈsempəns. In
rapid familiar speech, assimilations are also common at the
junctions of words: you will hear forms like ˈinnit (*isn't it*),
ˈwɔnnit (*wasn't it*), and ˈgim mi (*give me*). An example given by
Jones is it ˈkɑːmp bi ˈdʌn for *it can't be done*. This kind of change
is not likely to be carried over into other phonetic contexts: the
pronunciation kɑːmp for *can't* will only be heard before bilabial
consonants, that is, p, b, and m, not anywhere else: thus a
variant pronunciation has arisen, but is confined to certain positions, and the "normal" pronunciation kɑːnt is hardly likely to
be ousted by it.

Assimilations of the "coalescing" type are also taking place.
The group dj is often made into the affricate dʒ, as in *duke*
(djuːk, dʒuːk), *due* (djuː, dʒuː), *during, education*, and so on. Before
the War, the pronunciations with dʒ in these words were con-

sidered vulgar, but now they are quite common in educated speech, and are frequently used by B.B.C. announcers. Similarly, tj often becomes tʃ in words like *tube* (tjuːb, tʃuːb) and *Tuesday* (ˈtjuːzdi, tʃuːzdi); and sj becomes ʃ, as in *issue* (ˈisjuː, ˈiʃuː).

4. NEW WEAK FORMS

Many English words have two or more forms, a strong form and one or more weak forms; the weak forms occur only in unstressed positions, and are most frequent in rapid familiar speech; they are also normal, however, in slow familiar speech. As an example, the word *and* has a strong form ænd, and weak forms ənd, ən, nd, and n; it also has a weak form m which only occurs next to p or b, and a weak form ŋ which only occurs next to k or g. This is an exceptionally large number of weak forms for one word, but there are numbers of words with one or two weak forms, like *at* (strong æt, weak ət), *she* (strong ʃiː, weak ʃi), *should* (strong ʃud, weak ʃəd, ʃd), and so on. Some of the weak forms are recognised in spelling, like *don't*, *I'll*, *I'm*, and *he'd*: but many are not, and large numbers of speakers are unaware that they use weak forms in these cases.

Jones gives a list of more than sixty words which have weak forms differing notably from the strong forms. There are, however, a number of weak forms in common use which are not in Jones's list, and it seems probable that these have arisen (or at any rate spread much more widely in educated speech) since the list was compiled some decades ago. Examples of such weak forms, which are quite common in familiar speech, are given in the following phrases: srait (*that's right*); ˈsfʌni (*that's funny*); fjuˈlaik (*if you like*); ˈtsɔːl ˈrait (*it's all right*); ˈwɔts hiː ˈwɔnt (*what does he want?*). There we have s as a weak form of *that is*, f as a weak form of *if*, ts as a weak form of *it is*, and s as a weak form of *does*. This last form is particularly common, in expressions like *Who's he think he's talking to?*, *What's he think he's doing?*, *Who's he think he is?*, and *What's it matter?*

5. DIALECT-MIXING

Another factor that is probably affecting pronunciation is the dialect-mixing that has already been referred to: there is a

tendency for "popular" pronunciations of miscellaneous words
to filter upwards into R.P., or at least into educated regional
speech. An example is the word *heinous*, for which Jones's dictionary records only the pronunciation ˈheinəs; to-day, however, the pronunciation ˈhiːnəs is quite common even in educated speech. One whole group of popular pronunciations
which have become widely accepted in R.P. involves the sub-
stitution of a long vowel or a diphthong for a short vowel in
the first syllable of a polysyllabic word; examples of this are
homogeneous (ˈhou- for ˈhɔ-), *stabilise* (ˈstei- for ˈstæ-), *reproduce*
(ˈriː- for ˈre-), and *typography* (tai- for ti-). The pronunciations
with the short vowels already sound old-fashioned.

Some distinctively regional pronunciations also appear sporadically in R.P. One which seems to be fairly common is -eit
instead of -it in nouns and adjectives ending in -*ate*; the normal
tendency in R.P. is for the -it to be further weakened to -ət,
and the use of -eit is probably the result of northern dialect
influence (though in some cases it may arise by analogy with
verbs ending in -eit). Examples which I have heard from
otherwise normal speakers of R.P. include *Margate* as ˈmɑːgeit
and the noun *delegate* as ˈdeligeit; in R.P. these usually end in -it
(though in fact Jones does record an alternative R.P. form in
-eit for *delegate*). Other similar forms with "strong" endings
which are sometimes heard in what otherwise sounds like south-
eastern speech or R.P. are *mainland* (ˈmeinlænd for more usual
ˈmeinlənd), *necklace* (ˈnekleis instead of ˈneklis), and *Monday*
(ˈmʌndei instead of ˈmʌndi) (and so also with the other days of the
week). Such forms are probably the casual results of dialect-
mixing, and without any great long-term significance.

6. CHANGES OF STRESS

Changes are also going on in word-stress, and many of these
are in fact also a permeation upwards of popular pronunciations. In some cases, there are two possible ways of stressing
a word in R.P., and one of these is being reinforced by influence
from below. For *decade*, for example, Jones gives ˈdekəd as the
usual pronunciation in R.P., and diˈkeid as a less common
variant: but diˈkeid is the popular pronunciation, and seems to
be spreading upwards. Similar examples are *deficit* and *expli-*

cable: in these too the common R.P. pronunciation has first-syllable stress and the popular pronunciation second-syllable stress. There are other cases where the popular stressing is very rare in R.P., perhaps non-existent; such is the word *interesting*, which in R.P. is nearly always ˈintristiŋ; the popular form is ˈintəˌrestiŋ or ˌintəˈrestiŋ, and this is now very common in educated regional speech, and perhaps exists also in R.P.

In words of more than two syllables, the popular forms which are becoming acceptable in educated speech are forms with the main stress on the second syllable, where R.P. proper has the stress on the first syllable. In some of these words, the popular stressing may be due to analogy, or may at any rate be reinforced by analogy. For example, the popular pronunciation of *comparable* as kəmˈpɛərəbl may be due to the influence of the verb *compare* (on analogy with pairs like *detest/detestable*); in R.P., this word is ˈkɔmpərəbl. This kind of analogical stressing is also heard in *preferable*, *lamentable*, and *admirable*. However, there are many words where the second-syllable stressing of popular speech can hardly be explained by analogy; such, for example, are *doctrinal*, *communal*, *formidable*, *hospitable*, *pejorative*, *controversy*, and *aristocrat*. There are in fact various factors which affect the stressing of Romance loan-words and learned formations in English, of which analogy is only one. In all the words mentioned above, the forms with second-syllable stress are now heard in educated speech, though many of them are still not heard in R.P. proper.

In two-syllable words, the tendency seems to be the other way, that is, to move the stress from the second syllable to the first; this is the continuation of a historical process of long standing. Examples of words which in living memory were normally stressed on the second syllable in R.P., but which are now more often stressed on the first, are *garage*, *adult*, *alloy*, and the noun *ally*.

7. SPELLING PRONUNCIATIONS

There is another and important source of changes in pronunciation in Present-day English: the influence of the spelling. We have never had any thoroughgoing spelling-reform in Modern English (unlike some countries, which have reformed their

spelling by Act of Parliament), and our spelling is still essentially based on the pronunciation of late Middle English. In
consequence, our spelling is far from phonetic, and is not even
very consistent, so that there are sometimes quite wild discrepancies between spelling and pronunciation. It then sometimes happens that the pronunciation of a word is affected by
its spelling, because people say (or think) that the word ought
to be pronounced in such-and-such a way, because "that's the
way it's spelt." This is really a form of analogy.

The tendency to spelling pronunciation is encouraged by the
very size of the English vocabulary, which means that people
often meet words in their reading which they have never heard
pronounced; and by the large number of words in English borrowed from the classical languages, often learned words seldom
heard in ordinary speech but not uncommon in writing. It is
obvious that there will be a very strong likelihood of spelling-
pronunciations developing when there are large numbers of
words which will be seen many times in writing before they are
ever heard pronounced, so that the reader is obliged, as it were,
to devise his own pronunciation for the word when he encoun-
ters it. In our age, this tendency to spelling-pronunciations has
been further encouraged by universal and compulsory education, which has made us a nation of readers, and brought many
people into contact with words which they have never heard
spoken (in books, in newspapers, and in the forms they have to
fill in). Wireless and television are now no doubt altering this
situation somewhat, by restoring primacy to the spoken word,
but in the meantime a good deal has happened.

As could be expected, learned words often develop spelling-
pronunciations; indeed, such words often have many variant
pronunciations even within R.P., as a glance at Jones's *Pronouncing Dictionary* will show: for example *nausea* has four pronunciations, and *gaseous* has no less than eight. But there are
also many quite common words which have developed spelling-
pronunciations; in the following examples I give the traditional
pronunciation first and the new spelling-pronunciation second:
forehead (ˈfɒrid, ˈfɔːhed); *often* (ɔfn, ˈɔftən); *towards* (tɔːdz, təˈwɔːdz);
clothes (klouz, klouðz); *Ralph* (reif, rælf). For all these words
both pronunciations exist side by side, but the traditional pro-

nunciations of *clothes* and *towards* seem to be dying out. I remember a changeover to a spelling-pronunciation that occurred in my own speech when I was a boy; my father used a good traditional form for the word *waistcoat*, which he pronounced ˈweskit: but when I was at the grammar-school, and at the stage when my parents' speech was not good enough for me, I thought that ˈweskit was something to be ashamed of, and changed over to the spelling-pronunciation ˈweistkout, which seemed more refined. I now wish that I hadn't, but find that it's too late to change back, as this would merely feel like another affectation.

Spelling-pronunciations often arise when outsiders use the vocabulary of a specialised field. Insiders in such a field usually preserve traditional pronunciations, partly because the words are frequently used inside the group, but also because such usages help to mark them as members of the group. The importance of a special group-language in promoting feelings of cohesion can easily be seen if you look, for example, at an amateur dramatic society or a mountaineering club, where for the beginner the technical terms are one of the thrills of the business (marking him as an insider). One of the specialised fields where traditional pronunciations are very obviously preserved is that of seamanship, both professional and amateur; the man who goes sailing will set his ˈstʌnsl (if such a thing exists nowadays) and spit to ˈluːəd, whereas the armchair-sailor who only knows about it from books will see *studding-sail* and *leeward* and pronounce accordingly.

Newly-invented words are also liable to be given spelling-pronunciations, especially if they are of the kind that rely a good deal for their propagation on the press. I have noticed an example recently: *megaton*, which is a Greek-English hybrid, the second element being the ordinary English word *ton*; it means "having an explosive power equal to a million tons of high explosive," and is usually pronounced ˈmegətʌn. However, by people who do not realise its relationship with *ton*, and who possibly mistake the *-on* for a Greek ending, it is sometimes pronounced ˈmegətɔn, and I have more than once heard this pronunciation from B.B.C. announcers.

Another field where there has been a great extension of

spelling-pronunciations is that of place-names. For obvious reasons, the historical pronunciations of place-names are very tenaciously retained, however misleading the spelling may be: the name of your own village, and the names of the neighbouring places, are words which occur very frequently and which are learnt orally in early childhood. But this remains true only as long as communications are poor and people are not very mobile; once we reach the age of mass-media (especially newspapers) and social mobility, spelling pronunciations will appear: the name of a distant town, seen for the first time in a newspaper, will tend to be pronounced "as spelt." By the time the wireless and television became important, many such spelling-pronunciations were already well-established; and in any case the B.B.C. is not committed to traditional pronunciations for place-names, since these would often be puzzling and misleading for a newspaper-reading public. After some debate, for example, the B.B.C. adopted the pronunciation ˈdævəntri for *Daventry*, in preference to the local ˈdeintri.

There are many famous examples of English place-names where the spelling gives no idea of the historical pronunciation: *Hertford* (ˈhɑːfəd), *Greenwich* (ˈgrinidʒ), *Worcester* (ˈwustə), *Leicester* (ˈlestə), *Norwich* (ˈnɔridʒ), *Gloucester* (ˈglɔstə), etc.; in these, however, there is little likelihood of spelling-pronunciations developing, because they are too well known. But lesser-known places, like *Alnwick* (ˈænik), *Happisburgh* (ˈheizbrə), *Dalziel* (ˈdæljəl), *Covington* (ˈkʌviŋtən), *Wotton* (wutn), *Wrotham* (ˈruːtəm), and *Wreay* (riə) are almost certain to acquire a new pronunciation whenever they are referred to in a newspaper outside their home district, and in some cases this pronunciation may become widely disseminated.

You will all know of examples of this from your own experience. I will give a couple of examples from my own home-district, south Essex, which has been an overspill area for London during the last fifty years, and where, in consequence, the local dialect and traditional pronunciations have been very much swept away by off-Cockney. When I was a boy, *Romford* was still frequently ˈrʌmfəd, beside the innovation ˈrɔmfəd: but now the former is rare, especially among the younger generation (though the B.B.C. still uses it). A little further north is the valley of the *Roding,* along which lies a string of villages (High Roding, Abbess Roding, Margaret Roding, etc.), known collectively as The Rodings. How have you been pronouncing these names to yourself? When I was a boy, I heard (and still use) the pronunciation ˈruːðiŋ; this is in fact the historical form, but even thirty-five years ago the spelling-pronunciation ˈroudiŋ was common, and now that the Central Line has got there the ordinary Londoner who sees the name on an Underground diagram certainly says ˈroudiŋ. However, the last time I was in the district I noticed that White Roding announced itself on a large notice-board at the entrance to the village as *White Roothing:* so there are still some traditionalists dug in in the district.

It will be noticed that, in some of these examples, the new spelling-pronunciation is to some extent a reversion to an older pronunciation which has disappeared because of sound changes during the last thousand years or so: in *Daventry* there was once a v in the pronunciation, and in *Ralph* there was an l, but these were lost in M.E. or in early N.E., so that the modern spelling-pronunciations in fact involve a restoration of a lost sound. In other cases, however, this is not so: *Romford* for example did not originally have an ɔ in its pronunciation; it probably had an uː, which was shortened to u, which regularly developed into ʌ in the seventeenth century; the *o* in the spelling was simply a common Middle English way of denoting u, a habit which has led to modern spellings like *son* and *love.* In that case, it may be thought puzzling that Romford stands on the river *Rom,* which is always rɔm. The fact is, the name of the river is derived from the name of the town, and not *vice versa:* it is an example of *back-formation.* The name *Romford,* which probably meant originally something like "wide ford, roomy ford," was mistakenly imagined to mean "ford on the River Rom" (by analogy with places like *Dartford*), and the river accordingly was called the Rom; by this time, the pronunciation ˈrɔmfəd must have been common, and it was natural for the river to be called the rɔm.

The whole business of spelling-pronunciations must warn us not to underestimate the importance of the written language, and the extent to which it can react on the spoken language.

In the present century, there has been a strong tendency among linguists to insist that a language is something *spoken*, and that written language is only a secondary derivation from this. What was certainly learnt first by every user of a mother-tongue, and what probably came first historically in the creation of language by the human race, was speech; writing is only a graphical representation of speech, derived from it and translatable into it. It is important that the student should grasp clearly this primacy of the spoken language. When he has done so, however, he must then realise that, despite this fact, the written language has a certain life of its own. In modern literate communities like those of Britain and the United States, a speaker learns a very large part of his vocabulary from reading; and this is perhaps particularly true in Britain to-day, when large numbers of young people have greater educational opportunities than their parents had, and consequently move in fields of discourse to which they were not introduced by their homes. We all have passive vocabularies which are very large compared with our active vocabularies; and in our passive vocabularies there are usually many words which we have never heard spoken. Moreover, people who write at all fluently, or who are obliged to write by their occupation (like university students) usually have a much larger active vocabulary in writing than in speech. The basic structure of the language is of course learned through speech: but even here the written language can show variations of its own, especially in languages where there is a wide stylistic gap between speech and writing. The nonconformist preacher who improvises a prayer as part of his service very often uses the old second-person singular forms *thou* and *thee*, and the appropriate verb inflexions, when he addresses God; this is probably something that he has learnt from reading rather than at his mother's knee; the 1611 version of the Bible probably plays a large part here. In Swedish, there are special plural inflexions of the verb, both in the present and in the preterite, but these are never used in ordinary speech; they are used in a formal style of writing, and in highly formal speech (official orations, etc.); these forms are learnt from the written language, and are never mastered except by the highly literate.

8. CONTINENTAL PRONUNCIATIONS

I should like to call attention to one final kind of pronunciation-change in Present-day English: the tendency for words which look or sound "foreign" to acquire what one might call a "Continental" pronunciation. For example, the word *gala* can be either ˈgeilə or ˈgɑːlə; both these forms use ordinary English sounds, but the former has a normal kind of relation between spelling and pronunciation, while the latter has not. The traditional pronunciation is in fact ˈgeilə, and this is the only one given by H. C. Wyld (slightly old-fashioned) in his *Universal English Dictionary*. However, ˈgɑːlə is displacing it rapidly: it is given in Jones's *Pronouncing Dictionary* as the commoner of the two pronunciations, and is nowadays heard almost universally. It is pretty clear that the reason for the spread of this pronunciation is the knowledge that *gala* comes from the Italian; this knowledge is derived partly from the spelling and partly from associations of the word with Italian contexts. Of course, the word is not given a real Italian pronunciation: but it is pronounced with English phonemes which are felt to be the nearest to the Italian ones.

Such treatment is not confined, of course, to Italian words. The city of Gaza is nowadays nearly always called ˈgɑːzə, though Jones records only ˈgeizə; in a recent Third Programme production of *Samson Agonistes*, the pronunciation ˈgɑːzə was used throughout. For *armada*, Wyld gives only the pronunciation ɑːˈmeidə, which is so old-fashioned that I myself have never heard it; the normal form to-day is ɑːˈmɑːdə. Perhaps another example is the sub-standard pronunciation of *Copenhagen* (especially in a popular song about that city) as ˈkoupənˈhɑːgən, which has the disadvantage of being just as remote from the Danish pronunciation as from the traditional English one (which is ˌkoupnˈheigən).

Of course, ei is not the only sound affected. The word *proviso*, normally pronounced prəˈvaizou, is now sometimes heard as prəˈviːzou; Marlowe's *Faustus*, normally ˈfɔːstəs, is most often called ˈfaustəs by the present generation of students, through the influence of German; in the French loan-words *valet* and *beret*, pronunciations with -ei and -i are gaining ground at the expense of those with -it, and perhaps in *ricochet* -ei is

gaining ground on -et; for *chivalry*, the former pronunciation
ˈtʃivəlri is now almost dead, having been supplanted by ˈʃivəlri.
You will not find it difficult to add more examples to this list.

This process is in some ways the opposite of what one ex-
pects with foreign loan-words. The normal process is one of
naturalisation, an adapting of the word to native speech-habits.
Thus when the word *garage* was first borrowed from French, it
was quite possibly given a French pronunciation garaːʒ, with
French vowels and French uvular r: but this phase, if it existed
at all, must have been very short: almost at once the French
phonemes were replaced by the nearest English phonemes, and
the word given an English accentuation most resembling the
movement of the French; this produced the form gæˈraːʒ, which
is still occasionally heard. The process of naturalisation continued with the adoption of a more typically English stressing,
ˈgæraːʒ; the replacement of the rather rare ʒ by the commoner
dʒ, giving ˈgæraːdʒ; and, since long vowels are not very common in unstressed position, the weakening of aː to i, giving
ˈgæridʒ. The spelling no doubt played a part in these changes,
especially in giving the value idʒ to the ending -*age* (on analogy
with *mortgage, salvage*, etc.). In words which acquire a "Continental" pronunciation, on the contrary, a word which has
been naturalised in English, and which has undergone normal
historical processes of English sound-change, is made to conform more closely to the real or imagined pronunciation of the
foreign original.

One of the reasons for these Continental pronunciations is
no doubt the expansion of secondary and university education,
the greater number of people learning foreign languages, and
the great increase in foreign holiday-travel, which is no longer
the monopoly of the upper and upper-middle classes. I think,
however, that there is another cause as well: the changeover in
England from the old to the new pronunciation of Latin. Some
of the public schools still cling to the old pronunciation, but the
vast majority of people below middle-age who learned Latin
at school will have learnt the new. This new pronunciation,
moreover, is affecting the pronunciation of Latin words naturalised in English. A good deal depends on the frequency with
which the word or phrase is used: *Julius Caesar* is so well known

that he is always ˈdʒuːliəs ˈsiːzə when he is referred to in English, and is [ˈjuːlius ˈkaisar] only when we are reading Latin. On the other hand, I have often heard *Coriolanus* referred to in English as ˌkɔriəˈlɑːnəs, which, while not exactly the new Latin pronunciation, is probably the ordinary reader's approximation to it; the traditional English pronunciation is ˌkɔriəˈleinəs. It is hard, too, for people brought up on the new Latin pronunciation to use the traditional English pronunciation of phrases like *sine die*; no doubt lawyers all say ˈsaini ˈdaii, but an increasing number of young people feel uncomfortable at such an obviously "incorrect" pronunciation, and say ˈsiːnei ˈdiːei (which is again not exactly the new Latin pronunciation, but certainly an anglicisation of it). Similarly, the words *status*, *apparatus*, and *stratum* nowadays often have ɑː instead of ei in educated regional speech, though perhaps not in strict R.P. In *data*, however, the ei is still pretty well universal, perhaps because it is better naturalised in English (as is shown by its frequent use as a singular). In *quasi*, traditionally ˈkweisai, the new-pronouncers often go to a half-way house, and use the mixed form ˈkweisi, though ˈkwɑːsi and ˈkwɑːzi can also be heard. The word *deity*, traditionally ˈdiːiti, now sometimes becomes ˈdeiiti. And Latin plural endings in English words, which are normally anglicised (-*i* to ai, -*ae* to iː), are now often re-Latinised with the new pronunciation (-*i* to iː, -*ae* to ai): so that, for example, I have heard a B.B.C. announcer pronounce *nuclei* as ˈnjuːkliiː; the traditional form is ˈnjuːkliai.

Chapter III:

Notes and Suggestions for Further Reading

The best introduction to the phonetics of British English is Daniel Jones, *An Outline of English Phonetics* (8th edn., London 1956); I have also used the third edition (1932) and the sixth edition (1947). The same author's *English Pronouncing Dictionary* (London 1917, and many later editions) is indispensable for the foreign student of British English. Also useful for the overseas student is P. A. D. MacCarthy, *English Pronunciation* (Cambridge 1944). Miss Ida Ward, in *The Phonetics of English* (4th edn., Cambridge 1945), is more concerned with speech-training for the native speaker; she has many interesting examples of change going on in the language. A. C. Gimson's excellent book, *An Introduction to the Pronunciation of English* (London 1962), came into my hands too late for me to use it in the writing of this book; it is strongly recommended.

A useful introduction to English intonation is L. E. Armstrong and I. C. Ward, *Handbook of English Intonation* (Cambridge 1926). Later books on the subject are M. Schubiger, *The Role of Intonation in Spoken English* (Cambridge 1935) and R. Kingdon, *The Groundwork of English Intonation* (London 1958).

The British student would be well-advised to familiarise himself with these works on British English before turning to works on the phonetics and intonation of American English, as otherwise he may become confused, since much in the American analyses is not applicable to British English. This is the case, for example, in matters of stress; most American linguists distinguish four degrees of stress in English, which they say have phonemic significance; this seems to me to be just not true of British English; we have, it is true, a finely graded series of stresses, from strongest to weakest, but these are not all significant phonemically: for a phonemic analysis, I think that we only need to recognise *two* grades of stress in British English, strong and weak: we tend to achieve our effects of contrast and emphasis within the sentence by intonation-patterns rather than by stress-differences. American analyses, and further references, will be found in the American books referred to at the end of Chapter I (*e.g.*, W. Nelson Francis, A. A. Hill).

On the phoneme, see D. Jones, *The Phoneme* (Cambridge 1947), and K. L. Pike, *Phonemics* (Ann Arbor 1947). Some of the problems of the English phonemes are discussed by A. Cohen, *The Phonemes of English* (The Hague 1952). American linguists have produced extremely elegant analyses of the phonemic structure of English, but these once again are not entirely applicable to British English; for references, see the American authors referred to in the paragraph above and also B. Bloch and G. L. Trager, *Outline of Linguistic Analysis* (Baltimore 1942).

As explained in the text, the transcription I use in this chapter is a phonemic one, but at times I am in effect guilty of turning it into an allophonic one, when I discuss different members of a phoneme; in a book of this size it seemed impracticable to introduce two different transcriptions, and I have tried to phrase myself in such a way as not to be misleading; in addition, I enclose allophonic transcriptions in square brackets, *e.g.*, [ʊu]. For the analysis of R.P. into phonemes, I follow Jones, except that I treat pairs like u and u: as two phonemes, not one. I have also adopted Jones's method of marking primary and secondary stress, though (as I have said above) I think we could dispense with secondary stress.

For the phonological changes that have occurred during the New English period, see Vol. I of Otto Jespersen's *Modern English Grammar* (Heidelberg 1928), and J. Wright and E. M. Wright, *An Elementary Historical New English Grammar* (Oxford 1924). For the phonology of early New English, see the two large volumes of E. J. Dobson, *English Pronunciation 1500-1700* (Oxford 1957).

Anybody interested in following up what I have said about place-names and their origins should consult the volumes published by the English Place Name Society, which are done by counties, with various editors. A handy work for reference is *The Concise Oxford Dictionary of Place-Names*, by Eilert Ekwall (4th edn., Oxford 1960). A good readable introduction is P. H. Reaney, *The Origin of English Place-Names* (London 1960).

Chapter IV

The Growth of the Vocabulary

THE *New English Dictionary* (which I shall refer to simply as the *N.E.D.*) contains something like a quarter of a million words, not counting compounds and derivatives. Since the passive vocabulary of even a highly-educated Englishman is probably well under 150,000 words, and his active vocabulary very much smaller, you might think that the language was quite well supplied with words, and that we had no need of new ones. In fact, however, new words are being invented or introduced all the time. Sometimes a new word is produced by a single speaker only, in some special situation, and never occurs again; such a *nonce-word* has little importance. Sometimes a word produced by a single speaker is taken up by a small group, like the family, or a coterie of friends, or the staff of an institution, and persists there for a time without gaining any wider circulation; many small groups have such private words, and they rarely impinge on the community as a whole. Sometimes, however, a word is invented or introduced by a number of different people independently, because the social and linguistic climate favours this development, and such a word is much more likely to gain general acceptance. A new word, whether the product of one person or of many, may have the luck to be popularised by the press or the wireless, or to be adopted as a piece of exact terminology by some official body; or it may just spread through the community because it satisfies some need in the speakers, until it becomes an accepted part of the language, and eventually gets through to the lexicographers and is immortalised in a dictionary.

The rate at which the vocabulary changes varies from age to age. One period of rapid change in English was the fourteenth century, when vast numbers of French words were introduced into the language; another was the sixteenth century, when large numbers of new words were borrowed from Latin. In the nineteenth century there was a great expansion in the vocabulary of a specialised field, that of science and technology: the scientific vocabulary had been growing at an increasing speed throughout the seventeenth and eighteenth centuries, and in the nineteenth the flow of new words became a torrent. To-day we seem to be once again in a period of rapid vocabulary expansion. Some of the new words are names for new things, the products of modern technology: *nylon, sputnik, penicillin*; some arise from new concepts, especially in science: *neutron, quantum, phoneme*; some are the outcome of social change, of war, of new organisational forms and new social problems: *derequisition, firewatcher, blackmarketeer, beatnik*; some probably come from sheer linguistic exuberance and love of novelty: *super-duper* ("very good"), *skid-lid* ("crash-helmet"), *scram* ("depart").

In this chapter I shall give examples of new words in English. Many of these are not recorded in the *N.E.D.*; and most of those that are, are not recorded as occurring before the present century. There are a few exceptions, however: I have included some words which are recorded from earlier periods, but which have only become widely disseminated in the present century; and some which formerly existed in sub-standard usage or in some form of slang or cant, and which are now found in educated speech or writing.

Languages have many ways of acquiring new words, and I shall illustrate a number of these in giving my examples, though many of them are not important sources of new words in English at present. I shall not, of course, attempt to be exhaustive: this chapter is not meant to be a dictionary.

1. NEW LEARNED FORMATIONS

One very important group of new words in English in our time is that of the new learned words, especially scientific words. These are usually formed from Latin or Greek word-elements, especially from Greek: the proportion of Greek forms in our vocabulary must have increased very considerably in the last half-century. Many of these new scientific terms are highly specialised, and almost entirely unknown outside the small group of workers in the particular field. Reading through a scientific article in an unfamiliar field, I find many words which are strange to me—*anionic, chrondroitin, depolymerisation, desoxyribonucleic, dimerisation, metachromasy, monomer, nucleotide, thymonucleic,* and so on. There is no point in the layman's complaining that such an article is obscure: that would be rather like complaining that calculus is obscure, when you haven't learnt the multiplication-tables; to the specialist, no doubt, it is not obscure, but precise and unambiguous.

On the other hand, some of the new scientific vocabulary is known to the interested layman: the popularisers of science have given wide currency to words like *meson, neutron, positron, cyclotron,* etc., and (in another field) *allelomorph, chromosome, haploid,* etc. And then of course there are people with hobbies—radio-amateurs, amateur photographers, amateur naturalists, amateur engineers, and so on: because of such people, even more of the new vocabulary of science and technology circulates outside the narrow specialist sphere; and this is a phenomenon which will probably get more marked, because of the increasing emphasis on science in our educational system.

A certain number of the new scientific words, for varying reasons, gain an even wider circulation, and become part of the general vocabulary, known to people without any particular interest in science. *Television* has become a household word, for obvious reasons. Because of the importance of some radioactive isotopes for medical purposes, the word *isotope* has become widely known (though perhaps not all the people who use it could explain what it means). Many new drugs, similarly, are widely known because of their practical importance; the best-known, probably, is *penicillin,* and the general term *antibiotic* is also widely known. The word *transistor* is in common use, because the transistor has made possible very small wireless-sets, and this affects the man in the street. Words connected with nuclear energy also tend to get a wide circulation, because of the great importance of the subject both militarily and economically; examples are the words *reactor* and *moderator* in the new special senses they have acquired in this context.

One disadvantage of forming our new scientific vocabulary from classical roots is that such new words are opaque, that is, their meaning is not immediately apparent to the ordinary reader, as it might be if we formed such words from native elements; German linguists often point to this as a disadvantage in English compared with German. On the other hand, the words formed from Latin and Greek roots are more comprehensible internationally, which is of great importance for scientists. Moreover, we must not exaggerate the opacity of these words; it is true that, since the decline of the classics as the central subject in our educational system, they are less transparent than they were: but every scientist presumably gets to know the main Greek or Latin word-elements used in his particular branch, and thus becomes capable of understanding new words formed from them, and of forming them himself. Moreover, some of the commoner elements used in forming scientific words are now widely known and easily recognised by educated people, even when they know no Greek; I am thinking of elements like *tele, micro, mega, hyper, mono, iso, thermo, morph, gam, poly, scope, pod, pyro, phono, photo, neuro,* and so on. Knowledge of such elements helps the lay reader to learn and remember a scientific vocabulary.

2. AFFIXES

A second group of new words is those formed by means of living affixes, that is, prefixes and suffixes. Many of the new learned words, of course, are also formed with prefixes and suffixes; the difference is that the learned words are composed, as it were, on paper; one cannot imagine a scientist spontaneously inventing a new word like *metachromasy* in conversation: but one can easily imagine an ordinary English speaker inventing the word *deration* in conversation—indeed it is quite probable that this word was thus many times invented before it became official and printed. The ordinary English speaker, in other words, is familiar with the prefix *de-*, and understands its force; he will immediately understand a new word formed by adding it to some familiar root, and he may even be able to form such a new word himself in speech or in writing.

There are quite a few such living affixes in Present-day

English; here are some of the commoner ones, with examples of new words formed from them in our time. Most of these prefixes and suffixes are not of native origin, but come originally from the classical languages or from French: but this of course is of no importance, for they are now naturalised, and a part of the English language.

A. PREFIXES

de- (used with verbs in the sense of taking away, cancellation): *deration*, "remove from the list of rationed goods"; *degauss* (a word invented during the War to describe the process of treating a ship so that it would not detonate magnetic mines); *descale*, "remove scale (from a boiler)"; *decontaminate*, "remove the effects of contamination (*e.g.*, by poison-gas or radio-active materials)"; *derestrict*, "remove restrictions from"; *derequisition*, "return (a requisitioned property) to its owner." It will be noticed that many of these words arose directly from wartime and post-war conditions—rationing, magnetic mines, government requisitioning of property.

re- (repetition, putting back): this prefix can be used to form nonce-words with almost any verb or its derivatives, *e.g.*, *rethink*.

dis- (separation, division, negation): *disincentive*, "deterrent"; *disinfestation*, "removal of pests"; *disinflationary*, "causing economic disinflation."

un- (reversal of action, deprivation, negation): *unrationed*, "not rationed" (whereas *derationed* means "no longer rationed"); *unfunny*, "not amusing." This prefix (an original English one) is used spontaneously by speakers to form large numbers of nonce-words.

pre- (before in time): *prefabricate* (especially in *prefabricated houses*, "houses built from ready-made sections"); *precast* (concrete). Also used to form nonce-words, as in *pre-Hitler Germany*.

non- (negation): *non-operational*; *non-priority*; *non-utility*; *non-skid*, "designed to prevent skidding." This prefix can also be added spontaneously in speech to almost any adjective or noun (used attributively), to denote the absence of a quality.

self- (reflexive action, action independent of external agency): *self-searching*, "examination of own conscience"; *self-propelling*, (*e.g.*, gun); *self-sealing* (*e.g.*, petrol-tank); *self-correcting* (*e.g.*, machine, guidance-system); *self-starter*, "starter-motor of an internal-combustion engine"; *self-service*, "system whereby the customer (in a shop or restaurant) serves himself."

anti- (against): *anti-tank* (gun). This prefix too is used for spontaneous coinages in speech. If you dislike or disagree with your acquaintance Smith, you can say "I'm anti-Smith."

inter- (between): *inter-allied,* "between allies"; *inter-war,* "between (the two World) wars"; *inter-zonal,* "between zones."

B. SUFFIXES

-ise (forms verbs meaning "to act or treat in a specified way, to put into a specified state"): *miniaturise,* "design a very small version of"; *cannibalise,* "break up (an equipment) so that its parts may be used as spares"; *vitaminise,* "add vitamins to"; *finalise,* "make final, put into definitive form." From these verbs can be formed nouns in *-isation,* denoting the process: *miniaturisation,* etc.

-ie, -y (used for forming nouns, often with a diminutive-affectionate tone): *budgie,* "budgerigar"; *nappy,* "baby's napkin"; *clippie,* "woman bus-conductor"; *undies,* "women's underclothes"; *talkie,* "sound-film"; *goalie,* "goalkeeper"; *civvy,* "civilian."

-ist (nouns, denoting agent, or adherent of a doctrine or custom): *stockist,* "one who stocks (for sale) a specified kind of commodity"; *racialist,* "adherent of doctrines of racial superiority"; *leftist,* "adherent of the left (in politics)."

-ite (nouns, denoting a person connected with, an adherent of): *Hitlerite,* "supporter of Hitler"; *Bevanite,* "supporter of Mr Aneurin Bevan"; *socialite,* "person much involved in the life of high society and its values" (pejorative).

-ee (sufferer of the action): *detainee,* "person detained"; *evacuee,* "person removed from a place as part of an organised evacuation." This suffix is used for spontaneous coinages, often jocular.

-er (agent or instrument): *blockbuster,* "large bomb"; *firewatcher,* "person who watches out for fires during an air-raid"; *babysitter,* "person who looks after the baby while the parents go out"; *bumper,* "protective bar on motor-vehicle." This is a very active suffix, and many examples could be found.

-able (forms adjectives with a passive sense): *manoeuvrable,* "able to be manoeuvered"; *get-at-able* (ɡetˈætəbl), "accessible."

-ry (abstract or collective nouns): *rocketry,* "rocket-technology, things connected with rockets"; *circuitry,* "electric circuits."

This list is not exhaustive, but it will suffice to show how vigorous the prefixes and suffixes are in Present-day English word-formation.

Some purists object to new coinages when the elements are ultimately derived from different languages: this is the case, for example, with *precast*, where *pre-* is from Latin and *-cast* from Scandinavian, and with *stockist*, where *stock-* is a native English form and *-ist* goes back through French and Latin to Greek. It is difficult to see, however, why there should be any objection on principle to such hybrids; if a word-element is so well naturalised in English that people use it in forming new words, then it is in effect part of the English language, and its origins are irrelevant. Moreover, a strict application of this rule would abolish from the language a very large number of old and well-established words, such as *wrongful* (Scandinavian and English), *beautiful* (French and English), *countless* (French and English), *unveil* (English and French), *bearable* (English and French), *downward* (Celtic and English), *priesthood* (Latin/Greek and English), *devilry* (Latin/Greek and French), *churchman* (Greek and English), and thousands of others.

3. COMPOUND WORDS

New words can be formed by compounding, that is, by taking existing independent words and joining them together, as in *frogman* "man using light diving equipment," *bubble-car* "small motor-car with a transparent canopy," and *paperback* "book with a paper binding." But this raises the question, "What is a word?"; why should we not say that each of these is two words and not one? The answer depends on the way we care to define an English word. Many different definitions have been given; some of them are highly technical, and we cannot go into them here; it is worth considering, however, what factors influence the ordinary speaker in deciding what a word is; for we all have some views, however ill-defined, about what constitutes an English word and what does not; and no definition will be felt as satisfactory unless it conforms reasonably well with common usage. What criteria does the ordinary speaker use for deciding what constitutes a word?

In modern literate communities, the spelling has a great influence in determining the ordinary man's view: what is written as one word *is* one word. For many practical purposes this has much to commend it (though several ambiguities still lurk within such a definition), but it obviously does not get us to the root of the matter; for when we are faced with a new word like *bubble-car* or *frogman*, which has not yet got into the dictionaries, we in fact have to decide on its spelling; the journalist or the lexicographer must have some principles by which he decides to spell something as one word; and, since the written language is secondary and derived, there should be criteria in the spoken language by which he makes his choice. Moreover, even the dictionaries do not always agree with one another, and are not always consistent; one finds variant spellings like *greatcoat*, *great-coat*, and *great coat*; and we write *bedroom* as one word, but *bed-sore* with a hyphen; and are hyphened words to count as one word or as two?

Another factor that influences the ordinary speaker is the meaning; he feels that a word is in some way a unit of meaning, and his feeling about a compound-word may be influenced by its meaning; if the compound has a single meaning, or a special meaning distinct from that of its two parts, he will tend to call it a single word. Thus the meanings of *bubble-car* and *frogman* cannot be deduced from the meanings of their parts; similarly, a *redbrick university* does not necessarily consist of *red brick buildings*; and *a cupful*, which means "a (specified) measure," is felt as a single idea, in contrast with *a cup full*, which is felt as two. However, a little thought shows that this use of meaning as a criterion of the word is to some extent illusory. The phrase *bread and butter* denotes a single thing (with quite a different meaning from *butter and bread*), but nobody would find it satisfactory to call *bread and butter* a single word. The same is true of many other phrases, such as *the Prince of Wales*, *the Black and Tans*, *in spite of*, and so on. And conversely many compounds which the dictionaries print as one word are perfectly transparent, like *bedroom*, *firewood*, and *breastplate*.

The ordinary speaker may reply that *bread and butter* is not a single word because it contains more than one unit of meaning, and he may then be tempted to go on to define a word as the minimum meaningful part of an utterance. This will not do, however, for the noun-plural ending *-s* and the prefix *re-* and the suffix *-ee* are all perfectly meaningful, yet nobody would find it satisfactory to call them words. In fact, the minimum meaningful part of an utterance is what linguists usually call a *morpheme*; the plural ending -*s* and the affixes *re-* and -*ee* and the stem -*ceive* (as in *receive*) are called *bound morphemes*, because they cannot constitute an utterance by themselves, but only in combination with other morphemes; forms like *cup* and *full*, on the other hand, which can subsist by themselves, are called *free morphemes*. Compound words present a problem because they sometimes contain more than one free morpheme, and so are not minimum free forms.

It is possible, of course, to stipulate in your definition of a word that it shall not contain more than one free morpheme; in that case, compounds like *cupful* and *railway* have to be regarded as two words, not one, and are then best considered as *set phrases*. A serious disadvantage of this is that some such compounds become single words for some speakers, but set phrases for others; for example, *necklace* can be pronounced either ˈneklis or ˈnekleis, the latter being common in northern speech; the first pronunciation gives one free morpheme and one bound morpheme, whereas the second gives two free morphemes. It also has the result that *outrage* becomes two words, while *outrageous* remains one.

If set phrases occur very frequently, we in fact tend to regard them as single words. Thus we feel that *nevertheless* and *insofar* are single words (although each is compounded of three free morphemes) simply because we use them so frequently as single blocks of material. We are not always very consistent about this; for example, our dictionaries recognise *into* as a single word, but not *onto* (the Americans are more sensible about this). If we are to feel such a compound as a single word, then of course we must not be able to insert other words between the elements; we can separate the elements in *a cup full*, for example by saying *a cup brimming full*, but we cannot treat *a cupful* ("a measure") in this way; we can say *a young black bird* or *a black young bird*, but only *a young blackbird*. This of course is only a negative test.

Finally, and perhaps most important, there are purely phonetic or prosodic factors that make a speaker feel that a group of morphemes forms one word rather than two. The way the group is stressed is very important; if it has a single main stress, it will be felt as a single word. The difference is seen in *a cupful* (əˈkʌpful) and *a cup full* (əˈkʌpˈful); *black bird* (ˈblæk ˈbəːd) and *blackbird* (ˈblækbəːd). Historically, it seems, a phrase that is constantly used as a set-phrase tends to acquire single stress. Whether it acquires single stress because it is felt as a single word, or whether it is the other way round, is probably an unanswerable question, and so an unprofitable one. Obviously, however, the words must occur together frequently in some particular set of contexts for this to happen.

The word *greatcoat* is a modern example of a transitional state between a double-stress and a single-stress form: it has acquired a special meaning as a set phrase, and is now changing over to the stress-pattern for a single word. Jones gives three possible pronunciations for it: the one that he gives as the normal form in R.P. is ˈgreitˈkout; as a less common variant he gives ˈgreitkout; and as a third possible variant when the word is preceded by a stressed syllable he gives greitˈkout. It seems to me, however, that the second of these (*i.e.*, ˈgreitkout) is now the normal form, and that the other two are rare, and probably dying out; to me, at any rate, the form with double stress is quite unfamiliar. We here have an example of the historical process in action, a compound form taking on the stress-pattern of a single word.

If such a compound persists in the language, it may then undergo phonetic changes that make it quite indubitably into a single word. An example of this is *breakfast*. As the spelling shows, it was originally a compound of the free morphemes *break* and *fast*, but the vowel of the first syllable was shortened in early Modern English, and later the vowel of the second syllable was reduced to ə, and so we arrived at the present-day pronunciation ˈbrekfəst, in which neither element is the free form of a morpheme. Other historical examples of the process are *shepherd, cupboard, threepence, sheriff, stirrup, window,* and *fifteen*.

We cannot, of course, expect to see this process of fusion into a single word carried very far in the new compounds being formed in our own time. In most cases we shall find a pair of words used frequently together in a special sense; often we shall find that the pair has developed the characteristic single-stressing: but we shall not normally expect to find any decisive phonetic change. However, even this is not impossible: the new word *frogman* is usually pronounced in R.P. and in south-eastern Regional Standard (though not in educated northern speech) as ˈfrɔgmən; this is quite plainly a single word, for the form mən is not a free morpheme. There is a simple explanation for this, however: *frogman* has not been formed direct from the free morphemes *frog* and *man*, but on analogy with words like *postman* (ˈpoustmən), *policeman* (pəˈliːsmən), and so on. In effect, *frogman* has been formed from the free morpheme frɔg and the allomorph mən, which is a bound variant of the morpheme *man*.

Another case where a new compound is clearly a single word is the one where a shortened form is used for the first element; two examples of this come from the realm of automobile engineering: *con-rod* (ˈkɔnrɔd) "connecting rod" and *prop-shaft* (ˈprɔpʃɑːft) "propellor-shaft." The full forms of these are still only tentative candidates for wordship, but the abbreviated form *con-rod* is a fully-fledged word, since its first element *con* is not a free morpheme. The case of *prop-shaft* is less clear-cut since *prop* does exist as a free form as a shortening of *propellor*.

Most of the new compounds, however, have no such clear-cut claim to being words; what makes one think of them as single words is usually the distinctive new meaning acquired by the combination, often reinforced by the development of single stressing. An example of this is the very fashionable word *teddy-boy* (ˈtedibɔi); from meaning "youth who affects the wearing of Edwardian-style clothes" it has come to mean (by association) "youth who is unconventional, violent, and undisciplined, youth who dances rock-and-roll and admires pop-singers and hangs about on street-corners, young thug." The splash of meaning is wide, and it is hardly a transparent compound, but this very fact makes one feel it as a single word. This is a clear example of a word that has arisen in response to a new social phenomenon. Many of the new words arose from the War, for example from the technical apparatus of war; a remarkably large number have to do with aircraft and flying. There are many new compounds, for example, in *air*, some with single stressing (like *air-lift*, *air-strip*), some with double (like *air-taxi*, *air-umbrella*). Other words from flying are *pressure-cabin* (single stress) and *crash-landing* (double). The popular formations *buzz-bomb* (ˈbʌzbɔm) and *doodlebug* (ˈduːdlbʌg), both used of the German flying-bombs (V.1), no doubt had the effect of putting those frightening weapons in their place by making them comic, and thus reducing their terror. The seamier side of wartime and immediate post-war life is reflected in words like *black-marketeer* (where we have both compounding and a suffix) and *smear-word* (an outcome of the less reputable methods of political propaganda in the age of McCarthyism). The post-war interest in adolescents, which we have already seen in *teddy-boy*, is also seen in the widespread cult of the *teenager* (ˈtiːneidʒə) and things *teenage* (partly prompted by commercial motives, since adolescents now have more money to spend than ever they had before).

A type of compound-noun which is especially popular nowadays is that formed from a compound-verb (consisting of verb-plus-adverb): a *hand-out* (ˈhændaut), "official statement issued by an organisation to the press"; a *build-up* (ˈbildʌp), "concentration of forces or of effort, laudatory propaganda"; a *walk-out* (ˈwɔːkaut), "organised withdrawal of help or of labour, strike"; a *set-up* (ˈsetʌp), "arrangement, organisation"; and many others. These compound-nouns have single stress, whereas the verb-phrases from which they are derived have double stress (*to walk óut on somebody*, etc.).

So far, our examples of compounds have been nouns; however, there are also verbs, like the three very similar ones from flying, to *crash-land*, to *force-land*, and to *belly-land*. There are also new compound adjectives, as when we talk of a *long-playing* record; in American English, this is a *long-play* record, and this form (and others of its type) are now gaining some currency in England: I have seen *four-seat car* and *double-deck bus* (for more usual *four-seater* and *double-decker*). Another type of adjective, still rather slangy, is that formed from verb-plus-adverb; thus from the verb to *put off* ("disconcert, discourage") is formed the adjective *offputting* (ˈɔfˈputiŋ), "disconcerting, discouraging" (recorded by the *N.E.D.* as early as 1894). Somewhat similar is the repulsive adjective *sickmaking* (ˈsikmeikiŋ), "revolting, nauseating," which had quite a vogue a few years ago.

4. BLENDS

Blends, sometimes called *portmanteau-words*, are formed by combining some phonemes from one word with some phonemes from another, as in Lewis Carroll's "Jabberwocky," where he tells us that *slithy* means "lithe and slimy," and *mimsy* "flimsy and miserable." There are a few historical examples of blends in the English vocabulary; a pair of such examples is perhaps provided by the words *shriek* and *screech*; neither of these words corresponds exactly with any of the known possible ancestors in Old English or Old Norse, which could have been expected to produce modern forms like *ʃriː and *skraik and *skriːk, or (more hypothetically) *ʃraitʃ, but not skriːtʃ or ʃriːk. It is possible, therefore, that *shriek* and *screech* are products of blending, the skr- and -k being Scandinavian and the ʃr- and -tʃ English.

A modern example of blending is the word *brunch*, which is a combination of *breakfast* and *lunch*. The word *paratroop* ("parachute-troop") could be regarded as a blend of *parachute* and *troop*, but since the second word appears in it complete it is perhaps better regarded as a compound-word with shortening of the first element (like *con-rod*). However, the word *subtopia* is a blend, from *suburban utopia*; the *utopia* is ironical, for *subtopia* is a pejorative word used the describe the sprawling edges of our industrial cities and all that they stand for in our culture to-day: ribbon-development, petrol-stations, super-cinemas, advertisement-hoardings, road-houses, and architecture of the kind that Mr Osbert Lancaster has called "By-Pass Variegated." Another modern blend is *motel*, presumably from *motorists' hotel* (which is what it means), which we have imported from America; and yet another is *moped*, "motor-assisted pedal-cycle," which we have imported from the Continent of Europe. Typically English, however, is the recent formation *smog*, derived from *smoke* and *fog*.

5. SHORTENING

This has been a prolific source of new words in English. Usually the end of a word or phrase is lost, as when *public house* is shortened to *pub* (recorded from the mid-nineteenth century): but occasionally it is the beginning that goes, as when *omnibus* is shortened to *bus* (recorded from the early nineteenth century).

Any long word or phrase that comes to be much used in every-day speech is liable to be shortened; and there are plenty of examples in our own time.

Thus when *television* became a household-word after the War, it was very soon shortened to *telly* (ˈteli); normally the definite article is used with the shortened form but dropped when the full form is used (*I saw it on television*, but *I saw it on the telly*). Similarly, the intercommunication system on an air-craft becomes simply the *intercom* (ˈintəˈkɔm), a microphone is just a *mike* (maik), and a submarine a *sub* (sʌb). Women have a permanent-wave so frequently that they have shortened it to *perm* (pəːm). A learned medical word like *poliomyelitis* is not obvious material for the popular imagination to work on, but after the War this disease came into the news in Britain (as in other countries), and was very soon shortened to *polio* (ˈpouliou). Things that are both everyday and fashionable, like women's clothes, may provide good material for shortening; so in every-day speech a woman wears a *bra* (brɑː) rather than a *brassière* (ˈbræsiɛə), and *nylons* rather than *nylon stockings*. In this last case, as in some of the earlier ones, the original expression con-sists of a noun preceded by some epithet (an adjective like *public*, or a noun used attributively like *nylon* or *intercommunica-tion*): in such cases the original substantive noun is lost, and the attribute (either noun or adjective) becomes the new substan-tive expression, either in its full form (*nylons*) or shortened (*intercom*). Other examples of this process are the expressions *a pin-up*, meaning *a pin-up girl* "the kind of girl whose picture men pin up on the wall,"' and a *prefab* (ˈpriːfæb) from *a pre-fabricated house*. A similar example in which one of the words is reduced to its initial is *Three-D* (ˈθriːˈdiː), for *three-dimensional film*. An example where it is the first element of such an ex-pression that is lost is the use of *detergent* instead of *soapless detergent*; as a result of this change, the meaning of *detergent* is now commonly opposed to that of *soap*, whereas formerly it included it.

Sometimes quite a short and everyday word is shortened, as when *pepper* is shortened to *pep* in the special sense of "vigour, energy"; this in its turn has produced new compounds, like a *pep-talk* "a talk intended to ginger people up," and the new verb to *pep-up*, "invigorate, increase the intensity of"; this group of words is American in origin, but is now widely used in Britain.

We have already noticed examples of shortening occurring in one half of a compound; further examples of this are *pop-song*, "(particular type of) popular song," and *pop-singer*, "person who sings pop-songs." The terms *jet-prop* and *turbo-prop* to describe certain types of aircraft have the shortening in their second element, which is rather unusual, but it should be noticed that the form *prop* as a shortening of *propellor* had existed for a long time before these new compounds were formed (so long in fact that it sounded rather old-fashioned until given a new lease of life by these new forms: the sophisticated use *airscrew* rather than *prop* or *propellor*, unless they go in for slang and call it a *fan*).

It will be noticed that the pronunciation of these shortenings is often determined by the spelling rather than by the pronunciation of the full form: this is seen for example in *prop* (prɔp) from *propellor* (prəˈpelə), and *bra* (brɑː) from *brassière* (ˈbræsiɛə).

6. CONVERSION

This is another process which has for a long time been extremely productive of new words in English; it consists in the transfer of a word from one word-class to another, for example the use of a noun as a verb, or an adverb as a noun. This process has been particularly easy in the New English period, because of the way in which the language lost most of its inflexions in the Middle English periods; because of this, there are large numbers of words which, in the forms in which they commonly occur, provide no formal criteria for determining their word-class: by simply looking at a word like *lord*, we cannot tell what form-class it belongs to (whereas if we look at the Latin *dominus* we know quite well that it is not a verb, because of its ending); this makes it easier for a speaker to use *lord* (originally a noun) as a verb. The process of conversion in English has been especially vigorous between nouns and verbs; a typical example from earlier times is the pair of words *lead* (liːd) and *load*; these are related historically, but the first was originally only a verb, while the second was only a noun; from the first has come a new noun *lead* (liːd) (first recorded in 1300), and from the second a new verb, *to load* (first recorded in the late fifteenth century).

In our own time there are many examples of conversion. New verbs formed from nouns include to *contact* "get in touch with" (recorded in the nineteenth century, but not in this sense); to *steamroller*, "crush opposition, force a measure through by weight of numbers"; to *screen*, "project (a film), make a film from"; to *tape*, "record on a tape-machine"; to *feature*, "contain as a feature"; to *garage*, "place or keep in a garage"; to *service*, "carry out maintenance and repairs on (equipment or machinery)"; to *pinpoint*, "give exact location of"; to *vector*, "instruct (an aircraft) which way to fly"; to *bill*, "send a bill to"; to *streamline*, "make more efficient"; to *feather-bed*, "subsidise, protect from economic stress"; to *audition*, "give an audition to"; and many others. From the adverbial phrase *ad lib* "at pleasure, to any extent, without limit," has been formed the new verb to *adlib* (ˈædˈlib), "to improvise" (often used for example of an actor who forgets his part and extemporises).

Many of the new nouns formed by conversion are compound forms, formed, for example, from a verb-phrase. From the verb *to black out* (itself originally formed by conversion from the adjective *black*) comes the noun *blackout*; during the War this meant especially "the concealing of lights after dark"; this sense has fallen into disuse since the War, but the noun is still used in its other sense, "sudden loss of consciousness." Similar examples are the nouns *know-how* (ˈnouhau), "technical knowledge," and *hair-do*, "hair-style." In such cases, the double stress found in the verb-phrase is replaced by single stress in the compound noun: compare *I know how* (aiˈnouˈhau) with *I've got the know-how* (aiv ˈgɔt ðə ˈnouhau).

A new noun can also be formed from an adjective-adverb combination: thus a *high-up* is a person who is high up, that is, an important person, a high-ranking person; somewhat similar are the commonly used expressions of the type *the over-forties* ("the part of the population which is over the age of forty"), *the under-eighteens*, and so on. But the most remarkable new noun formed by conversion is not a compound; it is the form *a "must"* ("something indispensable"), formed from the auxiliary verb *must*. It is found mostly in sentences of the type *This is a "must,"* "This is something you simply must have (or do)," and is still usually put inside inverted commas. It is an expression that makes many people wince, but it has achieved a wide circulation, and is beginning to drop its inverted commas.

It is less easy to find examples of new adjectives formed by conversion. It is easy, indeed, to find nouns used attributively in a way in which they used not to be: typical examples are *key*, now commonly used to mean "essential, indispensable, of vital importance," as in *key man, key position, key component; utility* in the sense "made to a certain (austere and utilitarian) specification," as in *utility furniture; midget* in the sense "very small," as in *midget car, midget submarine*; and *top* in the sense "of high rank, at the top of their profession," as in *top model, top union-leader*. Although these words are now very commonly used attributively, one hesitates to say that they are adjectives; it is very common in English for nouns to be used attributively ("a *paper* cover," "the *hospital* staff"), but one does not regard such words as adjectives unless they fulfil other requirements (predicative use, use with adverb of degree, comparison); in fact it is useful to distinguish between word-class and function. We see the difference if we compare *midget* with *small*; we can say *a small submarine* or *a midget submarine*; we can also say *a smaller submarine* and *the submarine is very small*, but we cannot substitute *midget* for *small* in these cases. However, we are not always very consistent in our terminology, and it is quite common to call words like *paper, iron, steel,* and *copper* adjectives as well as nouns, simply because they are so frequently used attributively.

Also formed by conversion are many new compound forms used attributively, such as *teen-age*, "in the teens, to do with teenagers" (*teen-age clothes, a teen-age girl*); *backroom*, "not given publicity, working behind the scenes" (*the backroom boys, i.e.,* the research-workers and scientists who have done the basic work lying behind some achievement); *off-the-record*, "confidential, not to be publicly attributed to the informant" (*off-the-record information, an off-the-record talk*); and *round-the-clock*, "continuous, without intermission" (*round-the-clock attacks, a round-the-clock guard*). These, too, can hardly be called adjectives, but perhaps they are on their way to becoming them.

7. BACK-FORMATION

This is one of the curiosities of word-formation. It occurs when a word is wrongly imagined to be a derivative from some other (non-existent) form, and this hypothetical basic form is then invented and becomes a word in the language. An example of back-formation in English which is often cited (though it is not an absolutely certain one) is the verb to *beg*, probably derived by back-formation from the noun *beggar*. If this theory is right, the noun *beggar* is derived from Old French *begard*; in time, however, it came to be wrongly apprehended as a derivative form containing the agent suffix *-er*, and a verb to *beg* was accordingly created as the stem of this form. It will be seen that back-formation is in fact an example of analogy: the speaker knows pairs like *rob/robber* and *drink/drinker*, and when he hears the word *beggar* he makes it conform to the pattern by inventing a form *beg*. Another well-known historical example of back-formation in English is the verb to *sidle*, from the adverb *sidling*.

Back-formation is not of much importance in the growth of the vocabulary, but there are a few examples of its operation in our times. One is the verb to *automate*, "introduce automatic machinery into (an industry, a factory)," formed from the noun *automation* on the analogy of such pairs as *inflate/inflation, meditate/meditation*; the noun *automation* is itself a new word, presumably formed from *automatic*. Other examples are the verbs to *liaise*, "maintain contact with" (from *liaison*); to *enthuse*, "be enthusiastic" (from *enthusiasm*); and to *reminisce*, "talk about one's memories" (from *reminiscence*). These last two are recorded from the nineteenth century.

Perhaps we should also count as back-formations such compound verbs as *baby-sit, bird-watch, hedge-hop* ("fly very low"), and *mass-produce*; it seems probable that such verbs have not been formed direct, but are derived from verbal nouns like *bird-watching* and *hedge-hopping*; when, by constant collocation, such compound nouns have come to be felt as one word, a verb is then derived from them by back-formation.

8. REVIVALS

Another very minor way in which the vocabulary has been helped out in our time is by revivals; obsolescent words, which are dying out because the object they denote has itself died out, are given a new lease of life by being given a modern application. Thus before the War, *frigate* and *corvette* were dying words, found only in historical contexts as technical terms for two types of ship long out of use: but during the War the Admiralty revived these words and applied them to two new types of ship, so that they once again have a general currency. Somewhat similar is the revival of the word *armour*, which has come to be used as a general term for tanks and armoured vehicles ("Field-Marshal Montgomery's armour advanced to the Meuse . . . "); in this way a word can be taken out of the museum and put back on the battlefield.

9. PROPER NAMES AND TRADE NAMES

Another minor, but interesting, way in which the vocabulary is expanded is by the adoption of proper names and trade names as common nouns. An example of a proper name which has become firmly established as a common noun in our time is *diesel*; the *diesel-engine*, often shortened to *diesel*, takes its name from the German inventor Rudolf Diesel, who first demonstrated it in the closing years of the nineteenth century; now it is so well established that it has given rise to numerous compounds (*diesel-oil, diesel-fuel, diesel-powered, diesel-train*); moreover, one of these, *diesel-train*, has now itself undergone shortening to *diesel*, so that people commonly say *I came over by diesel* (or *on the diesel*). Another example, but one that will perhaps prove less tenacious, is *quisling* ("a traitor, one who collaborates with the enemy"), formed from the name of the Norwegian who collaborated with the Germans in their occupation of his country; the spread of this word as a common noun was probably helped by its formal characteristics: the suffix *-ling* occurs in English nouns (*fledgling, sibling*, etc.), and so the word fitted easily into the familiar patterns of the language. A third word was provided by Mae West, the luxuriously-built American film-star; during the War, a *Mae West* (ˈmei ˈwest) was the jocular name given by airmen to their inflatable life-jackets, and this became so widely accepted that ultimately the Air Ministry adopted it as an official name.

Trade names are also adopted into the language occasionally, but the extent to which this happens is often exaggerated. A good example is *thermos-flask*, now commonly used as a generic term for vacuum-flask. Some dictionaries (*e.g.*, Wyld's *Universal English Dictionary*) give the word *kodak* as a common noun meaning "small hand camera"; this may have been true for a short time when the small Kodak cameras first had a big break-through on the market, but it is certainly not true to-day: if you tell a friend that you have bought a new Kodak, he will be somewhat baffled if you then add that it's a Leica. Both Wyld and the *N.E.D.* also give *kodak* as a noun meaning "a photo-graph taken with such a camera," and as a verb meaning "to take photographs with such a camera," but these must have been usages with a very short life, for they are never heard to-day. Other cases which are sometimes cited are *Hoover* ("vacuum-cleaner"), *Frigidaire* ("refrigerator"), *Biro* ("ball-point pen"), and *Bendix* ("washing-machine"): but none of these words has more than a very doubtful claim to being a common noun. The likeliest, perhaps, is *hoover* as a general word for "vacuum-cleaner," with an accompanying verb *to hoover*; these are heard from a number of people, but they are a minority, and (because of the large number of makes of vacuum-cleaner on the market) a dwindling minority; more-over, the Hoover washing-machine is now as well-known as the Hoover vacuum-cleaner. For a short time the word *biro* did look like succeeding as the normal word for "ball-point pen," but as more makes came on the market this usage became rarer, and the normal term to-day seems to be *a ball-point*. The word *bendix* is rarely used as a generic term for "washing-machine": once again, the competition from other makes is too strong. And *frigidaire*, finally, seems to have very little claim to be a generic word for "refrigerator," at any rate in this country; the ordinary popular word is *fridge* (fridʒ), which is perhaps a shortening of *refrigerator*.

Strangely enough, nobody seems to have pointed out one clear example in present-day English of a trade-name which has become a common noun—perhaps because it is so well naturalised that they don't realise that it *is* a trade name. I am referring to the everyday name for the small paraffin pressure-stove, which operates by vapourising the paraffin by the heat of its own jet. When I was issued with some of these during the War, they were called by the quaint official name of "Stoves, wickless, paraffin": but when I looked at them, I found that they were simply ordinary *primus-stoves*. And *primus-stove* (ˈpraiməs stouv), or simply *primus* (ˈpraiməs), is what these stoves are called by the thousands of campers, walkers, and mountaineers who use them. But *Primus* in this context is a trade-name, the property of the Swedish firm which first put such stoves on the market. The shopkeepers who sell them of course know this, and are careful to distinguish between the Primus and other makes (Optimus, Phoenix, etc.): but the ordinary camper goes on using the word *primus* for them all. This word, oddly enough, does not occur in Wyld's dictionary.

10. INITIALS

This is another minor source of new words: with the ramification of bureaucracy and the growth of bigger and better organisations, more and more sets of initials come into use, some in limited spheres, some widely. Most of these remain proper names, but a few have developed into common nouns.

Some sets of initials retain their pronunciation as initials, like *the B.B.C.* (ðəˈbiːˈbiːˈsiː), "the British Broadcasting Corporation," and *I.T.V.* (ˈaiˈtiːˈviː), "Independent Television." As common nouns we have *a V.I.P.* (əˈviːˈaiˈpiː), "a very important person," and *on the H.P.* (ɔn ðiˈeitʃˈpiː), "on the hire-purchase (system)," both with a wide circulation.

Others develop a kind of spelling-pronunciation, and then very often are no longer written as initials. An example of this is *radar* (ˈreidɑː), from the initials of "radio direction and ranging." This was originally an American form; the British equivalent was R.D.F., standing for "range and direction finding," but the American term was adopted instead during the War, as part of a programme of standardisation of Allied technical terms. Recently, the word *radar*, which was originally an uncountable, meaning "a certain *system* of aircraft detection" (as in *the aircraft was tracked by radar*), has come to be used as a countable (*a radar*), meaning "a radar-set, a radar-station." Other examples of this kind of spelling-pronunciation are *the Naafi* (ðəˈnæfi), "Navy, Army, and Air Force Institutes," which is the normal name in the forces for the official canteen; and *Unesco* (juːˈneskou), "United Nations Educational, Scientific, and Cultural Organization."

Some sets of initials exist in both forms: thus the Royal Air Force can be either *the R.A.F.* (ðiˈɑːˈreiˈef) or (more slangily) *the Raf* (ðəˈræf); and the United Nations (Organisation) can be *the U.N.* (ðəˈjuːˈen) or *Uno* (ˈjuːnou).

11. LOAN-WORDS

One of the major sources of new words in English in the past has been borrowing from other languages; indeed, we have been so hospitable to foreign words that our vocabulary contains more words of foreign origin than of native stock. The three major sources of our borrowings have been Scandinavian, especially in the late O.E. and early M.E. period; French, especially in the M.E. period; and Latin, especially in early New English: but borrowing has not been confined to these periods, and a score of languages have contributed in varying degrees. In the present period, loan-words are not of much importance for the expansion of our vocabulary: we are exporting words rather than importing them. Many of our new scientific and technical words are formed from Greek or Latin morphemes, but they are new coinages, not loan-words; the older scientific vocabulary does indeed include a few words lifted intact from the classical languages (*focus, nucleus, stigma, thorax*), but this is no longer usual: most of our new scientific words are constructed, not borrowed.

Small numbers of words, however, are still drifting into English from other languages. French has declined a good deal in cultural prestige in the last half-century, but a knowledge of spoken French still has enough snob-value in Britain for a good many French words and phrases to get used in educated English speech, though many of them never become naturalised. Indeed, it may be the very prestige of a good French accent that hinders their naturalisation: there are French words like *penchant* and *tête-à-tête* which have been floating about in

English since the late seventeenth century, but which are still felt as foreign, and are still spoken with a somewhat French accent. A more recent phrase which has had some vogue is *de nos jours*, and there are others of the same kind. As might be expected, a number of the recent loans from French are from the fields of fashion and of the arts: *pointillism* (1901), *démodé* "out of fashion" (1896), *couture, montage, collage* (these three not in the *N.E.D.* Supplement). The word *avant-garde* has been borrowed again, in a figurative sense (of artists, intellectuals, etc.): it is found in earlier times in English, but only in its literal military sense of "vanguard" (which is itself yet an earlier borrowing of the same word). French words from other fields include *questionnaire, garage,* and *chauffeur* (all early twentieth century).

Other words have come in from German during the two World Wars: during the First World War, the verb *strafe* was adopted, in the sense "to shell or bomb heavily," from the German verb *strafen* "to punish." A similar loan during the Second World War was *blitzkrieg*, quickly shortened to *blitz* (blɪts); the German *Blitzkrieg* meant "lightning war," a very appropriate word for German methods of warfare in their Polish and French campaigns of 1939-40, but in the English mind the word came especially to be associated with the heavy German air-raids on Britain in 1940-1; *the blitz*, therefore, came to mean "the air-raids," and later, when the heaviest period of raids had passed, it came also to mean "the period in 1940-1 when the air-raids were at their height," so that people could be heard to say such things as *During the blitz I was living with my mother in the country*. Another German word that came into use in England during the First World War, and which was given a new vogue by the Second, was *ersatz*, popularly pronounced ˈɛəzæts or ˈɛəsæts or ˈəːsæts, and most often used attributively in the sense of "synthetic, not genuine" ("ersatz rubber," etc.), usually with an implication of inferiority to the genuine article. Various German technical terms of war were also used, especially by the troops, for example *teller-mine* ("disc-mine, anti-tank mine"), but these have not survived in the post-war language. Another sphere from which German words have recently entered English is that of psychology: the word *angst* (æŋst) ("fear, anxiety") is now firmly established in intellectual circles, and *schadenfreude* ("pleasure in the troubles of others") is sometimes heard, though it is hardly naturalised yet. From the sphere of politics comes the word *realpolitik* ("realistic policy"), also quite often heard in intellectual circles, though this too is still felt as a foreign word.

Recent loan-words from other languages have usually been the result of specific events or situations which have caught the public eye. From Afrikaans comes *apartheid*, to describe the racialist policies of the South African nationalists; in England, this is a pejorative word. From Russian come *sputnik* ("artificial earth satellite") and *lunik* ("space vehicle aimed at the moon"); these words, however, are used only of *Russian* space-vehicles; American ones are usually called *satellites*, or (if they are not being put into orbit round the earth) *space-vehicles* or *space-probes* or just *probes*. This is rather similar to the limitation in application of the word *U-boat*; this word was formed during the First World War on the pattern of the German *Unterseeboot*, and it was used only of German submarines, not of British ones; this usage continued during the Second World War: German submarines were called *U-boats*, and so, occasionally, were other enemy ones (Italian, Japanese), but British ones were always *submarines*.

Recently I have seen in the English press two words from the realm of sport which probably come from Swedish, which is rather unusual: they are *orienteering*, from Swedish *orientering* ("cross-country racing with map and compass") and *motocross* ("cross-country motor-cycle racing"). Whether or not these words survive in English will probably depend mainly on the extent to which the sports take on. Another Swedish loan-word, now well-established, is *moped* "motor-assisted pedal-cycle." This is now the normal west European word for this machine, but it originated in Sweden: it was invented by Mr Harald Nielsen, editor of the Swedish periodical *Motor*, and was launched as an avowedly new coinage in that periodical's sixth number, on 9 February 1952. Later, the word won a competition held in Germany for naming the machine, but was then admittedly borrowed from Swedish.

Another type of loan from a foreign language is the *calque* or *loan-translation*. In this case, the word is not taken bodily into the borrowing language: instead, native equivalents are found for its various elements; thus on the pattern of English *loudspeaker* has been formed the French *haut-parleur*; and the English word *loan-word* is itself a loan-translation from the German *Lehnwort*. In recent years English has made a number of loan-translations from the German. Some of these are from the realms of politics and war: *shock-troops* is from the German *Stosstruppen*, and *power-politics* from *Machtpolitik*. Another sphere in which English has translated German words is that of psychology, especially psychoanalysis; this is not surprising when you consider that the founders of the main schools of psychoanalysis all wrote in German; when their works were translated into English, the translators tended to translate the German technical terms into English compound nouns or phrases: so *Minderwertigkeitskomplex* became *inferiority complex*, and *Wunschdenken* became *wishful thinking*.

12. INTERNAL LOANS

These are the words borrowed from other dialects of the same language: borrowed, for example, by the standard language from regional or class dialects, or from the specialised vocabulary of occupational groups (lawyers, actors, miners, etc.), or from the many varieties of slang or cant.

One aspect of this is the commerce in words between Britain and the United States, in which Britain is mainly an importer. Where America and Britain have different words for the same thing, the American word is now often heard in Britain alongside the British word: American *radio* beside British *wireless*, *movie* beside *film*, *canned* beside *tinned*, *gas* beside *petrol*, *gas-pedal* beside *accelerator*, *elevator* beside *lift*, *rugged* beside *robust*, *automobile* beside *car*, etc.; of these, *radio* is the only one which is seriously threatening to displace the British form. Other American words are adopted because there is no British equivalent, or because their flavour catches the fancy: *jazz*, *blurb* "commendatory advertisement on wrapper of book," *cagey* "cautious, non-committal," *gimmick* "small device used by a conjurer in performing a trick (also figuratively)," and so on; the first two of these are firmly established, the other two are recent and may have only a temporary vogue.

Inside Britain, there is not much sign that regional dialect-words are making their way into the standard language: rather, the words of the standard language are displacing regional dialect words. There are a few examples, however, of the former process: one is the adjective *gaumless* (ˈgɔːmlis), "stupid, dim-witted"; as a boy living in the south-east of England I never heard the word, but in the last twenty years it has become fairly common, and has pretty clearly spread from the northern dialects; it is not a new word, for the *N.E.D.* records it from the eighteenth century, but always in regional dialect contexts. The absence of a literary tradition for the word is shown in the doubts about its spelling: modern writers often spell it *gormless*. Another example is *gaup* (gɔːp), which exists in a number of regional dialects and is presumably a variant of *gape*; it has also gained some currency in recent years. But these are isolated phenomena.

Slang and cant have been more influential, and have been spread widely by the armed forces during the two World Wars. One slang army expression which has gradually spread to the rest of the community is *eyewash*, "humbug, something intended to deceive"; the word is not a new one, but formerly was used in the standard language only in its literal sense of "eye-lotion." Another army word which has spread widely is the verb to *scrounge* "acquire by doubtful means, steal," a word which has regional dialect origins; in the Second World War it was commonly used (at any rate in the R.A.F.) to mean "dodge work, malinger," but this meaning has not gained any wide currency. Some army-slang is borrowed from foreign languages with which the army has had contact, especially Eastern languages; one such word which has spread widely is *buckshee*, "free, extra," which is borrowed from Hindi. Some service-words with more technical meanings have also become widely known, such as the R.A.F. words to *scramble*, "order (aircraft) to take off," and to *buzz*, "fly very close to, make a mock attack upon (another aircraft)."

The two World Wars, too, have probably helped to spread Cockney rhyming-slang, and although none of its usages have been accepted by R.S., they are now widely understood all over the country. Well-known examples are *trouble and strife*, "wife"; *half-inch*, "to pinch, steal"; and *titfer* (ˈtɪtfə), a shortening of *tit for tat*, "hat."

The verb to *wangle*, "accomplish something in an irregular way by scheming or contrivance," was also current in the armed forces during the two Wars, but originally it seems to have been printers' slang; the *N.E.D.* first records it in 1888. The noun *gadget*, "small tool, contrivance, or piece of mechanism," is first known as sailors' slang in the late nineteenth century; it spread into the general language in the present century. The word *spiv* comes from the language of race-gangs, where it is first known in the eighteen-nineties; it spread in the general language with explosive suddenness at the end of the War, when it was used to denote a particular social phenomenon of that time—the man who lived by his wits by means of dubious transactions, especially on the black market.

Words are also penetrating to the general language from the coffee-bar and jazz-club slang of adolescents, and will probably spread even more as the adolescents grow up. Most of this language is still a mystery to the greater part of the population over the age of twenty, but odd words drift through the age-barrier: so that most people have come across expressions like *a square*, "a person who doesn't like jazz, a stuffed-shirt," the adjective *hip*, "belonging to the group, worthy of adolescent approval," and the verb *to dig*, "to agree with, appreciate, understand."

13. SUMMARY

In summary it can be said that the majority of new words in English to-day are being formed from our existing resources, not borrowed from abroad. The methods of word-formation especially productive in our time are affixation, conversion, and the making of new compounds. Moreover, large numbers of new words are being constructed from classical word-elements, particularly Greek, mainly as technical terms in science and technology. Very few words are being borrowed from foreign languages, compared with previous periods of the language.

Loss of Words

While new words are being introduced, other words are always being lost from the language. It is less easy to point to these words than to the new ones, because words usually die slowly, and it is difficult to be sure of the exact moment when one has gone: it may linger on in certain styles of writing or among certain groups of the community long after it has fallen out of general use. Moreover, a word that at one time seemed practically dead may be revived; for example, Wyld says in his dictionary (1936) of the word *lollipop* that it is "now hardly in actual use among any class of speakers in England"; since the War, however, this word has come into use again. Other words die out from speech but remain in use for a long time in writing, and even when they are rarely written remain known to people from older writings; here the Bible, the Prayer Book, and Shakespeare play a considerable part. Some obsolescent words are given a new lease of life by the newspapers, which like to have short words for headlines: thus the verb to *wed* is commonly used in newspapers ("Duke's Son Weds Top Model"), but is never heard in speech, where the ordinary word is *marry*; the newspapers are helped here by the fact that the word *wedding* is in everyday use, so that *wed*, though archaic, is readily understood. It is difficult, therefore, to pick on certain words and say that they have finally died out from the language in our time; though we can be certain that numerous words now familiar to us will be quite archaic in a couple of hundred years time.

Some linguists have suggested that one cause of loss of words from a language is homophony, that is, the existence of different words with the same sound; because of the possibility of confusion, it is argued, one of the words falls out of use and is replaced by a synonym. This argument has some force for cases where the two homophones can occur in similar contexts, so that there can be real ambiguity. Thus, when by the process of phonetic change the words *queen* and *quean* (originally pronounced differently) had become homophones, there obviously was the likelihood of confusion between them, and this may well have contributed to the disappearance of *quean*; and similarly with the verbs *let* "permit" and *let* "prevent, obstruct," the second of which is found in Shakespeare but has since disappeared from the language. On the other hand, some pairs of homophones which have been suggested for this process are not in fact at all plausible: it is hardly likely that *ail* has fallen out of use because of its homophone *ale*, since it is difficult to imagine a context where the two could be confused: and similarly with *wight* (*white*), *ay* (*I, eye*), *nay* (*neigh*), and *raze* (*raise*), though a case might be made out for this last pair.

Another cause of loss is that short forms are preferred for words which occur at all frequently, so that a long word is likely either to be shortened or to be replaced by a shorter synonym or near-synonym: the word *aeroplane* is not likely to have a long life in our age of air-travel, and is already commonly replaced by the shortened form *plane*. On the other hand, it sometimes happens that the processes of phonetic change make a word so short that it is felt to be insufficiently distinctive, and so is either replaced by another word (as Old English *ea* was replaced by the French word that has become our *river*), or is reinforced by the addition of further material to it (as in P.E. *magpie* for earlier *pie*). But no simple explanation can be given for most of the words that fall out of the language; the causes are many, and often obscure.

It is perhaps worth calling attention to one particular type of word which is falling into disfavour to-day, especially with women: this is the sex-discriminating word used to indicate that the member of some profession or the holder of some office is a woman. An example is *authoress*; *author* has no special sex-implication, and can be used of both men and women; this is called the *unmarked* member of the pair; whereas *authoress* is a less general word, and makes a special point about the sex of the writer; this is called the *marked* member of the pair. Where such pairs of words exist, women nowadays tend to avoid and dislike the use of the marked member, presumably because it seems to imply that there is something unusual about a woman being in such a profession or office. Thus a woman will tell you that she is a *poet* rather than a *poetess*, an *editor* rather than an *editress*, a *chairman* rather than a *chairwoman*, and a *teacher* rather than a *woman-teacher*; she will probably find *lady-teacher* insufferably pretentious. There are of course cases where the "feminine" form is still always used, like *actress*, *waitress*, and *stewardess*, but it will be seen that these are not in fact marked members of a pair: the forms *actor, waiter*, and *steward* are not general terms like *author* and *chairman*, but are as strictly limited to men as their "feminine" forms are limited to women.

Another linguistic consequence of the achievement by women of political equality with men is that certain words designating posts and offices, originally used only of men, are now used also of women, sometimes with an odd effect. A good example is *Lord Mayor*; in the old days, the Lord Mayor of a city was always a man; his wife was the *Lady Mayoress*; she had no official or administrative functions, but certain social ones. Nowadays it is not at all unusual for a woman to become the civic head of a city, and then of course she must still be called the Lord Mayor (not the Lady Mayoress); the social functions of the Lady Mayoress are then carried out by some other woman specially appointed to the position by the Lord Mayor (usually her sister or mother). This is by no means an imaginary case: in Leeds, for example, two recent Lord Mayors have been women.

Chapter IV:

Notes and suggestions for further reading

For the development of the English vocabulary, see the various histories of the English language already mentioned. There are also a number of books specifically on the English vocabulary; a number of popular ones have been written by Ernest Weekley, beginning with *The Romance of Words* (London 1912). Particularly useful are J. A. Sheard, *The Words We Use* (London 1954), and M. S. Serjeantson, *A History of Foreign Words in English* (London 1935). For the specialist, there are a few detailed monographs on particular aspects of the growth of the vocabulary, like E. Björkman's *Scandinavian Loan-Words in Middle English* (Halle 1900-2).

The standard work of reference for the history of any normal modern English word is of course the *N.E.D.*, that is *A New English Dictionary on Historical Principles*, edited by J. H. Murray and others (10 vols. and Supplement, Oxford 1888-1933). It was reissued in 1933 under the title *The Oxford English Dictionary*. Two works of lexicography which illustrate the rapid expansion of the English vocabulary in our time are P. C. Berg, *A Dictionary of New Words in English* (London 1953), and R. W. Zandvoort and others,

Wartime English (Groningen 1957); Berg's book, however, should be used with caution: it contains quite a few words which are not really new at all: for example, both *denationalise* and *re-educate* are well over a century old. For dialect-words, see J. Wright, *English Dialect Dictionary* (London 1898-1905), and for slang and cant see E. H. Partridge, *A Dictionary of Slang and Unconventional English* (London 1937). On the rise of the scientific vocabulary, see T. H. Savory, *The Language of Science* (London 1953).

On the morpheme and the word, see the works on general linguistics given at the end of Chapter I, and also E. A. Nida *Morphology* (Ann Arbor 1949).

For an introduction to the concept of marked and unmarked forms, see *The Teaching of English*, edd. R. Quirk and A. Smith (London 1959), pp. 39-44, 185-6.

For the information on the origin of the word *moped*, I am (indirectly) indebted to Professor Gösta Bergman, of the Institutet för Svensk Språkvård.

Those who are unfamiliar with "Bypass Variegated" and the other architectural growths of Subtopia will find them splendidly depicted in Osbert Lancaster's book *From Pillar to Post* (London 1938).

Chapter V

Changes in Meaning

WORDS often develop new meanings, and when they do, they sometimes lose their old meaning. When during the Modern English period, *presently* came to mean "fairly soon," it gradually lost its earlier meaning of "immediately"; when *wan*, during the late Middle English period, came to mean "pale," it did not long thereafter retain its earlier meaning of "dark"; and the reason for this is pretty obvious, since the co-existence in one word of such contradictory meanings could lead to misunderstanding; semantic conflict tends to lead to loss of a meaning. In other cases, however, the old meaning often continues to coexist with the new, and we get the phenomenon of multiple meaning, or polysemy; for example, when *collation*, meaning "the act of comparing," acquired in the fourteenth century the new meaning "a light meal," both meanings were retained. Sometimes, when a word acquires two very different meanings, it comes to be apprehended as two different words, which may then be distinguished from one another by spelling: this has happened with *flour* and *flower*, *metal* and *mettle*. Some words develop large numbers of new meanings, branching out along a number of different lines; because such words have been heard in many different kinds of context, they have large numbers of possible associations for the hearer, and can be used to produce complex effects. If you look up in a large dictionary such words as *sense*, *nature*, *reason*, and *good*, or even everyday verbs like *put* and *get*, you may begin to wonder how we manage to use language at all. In fact we manage pretty well, because the context has the effect of narrowing down the possibilities; in the referential use of language, for example in scientific writing, this selective process is very strict, since clarity and unambiguity are essential: but in some uses of language, and notably in poetry, deliberate use is made of the associations clustered round words because of polysemy, to suggest ambivalence or complexity of attitude.

There are various causes of change of meaning, some social, some psychological, some purely linguistic, and various types of classification of semantic change have been proposed. Some systems proposed have been purely logical, some psychological; some have been mainly concerned with the inception of a new meaning, others with its spread; some have had only three categories, others a dozen or more. The late Gustaf Stern, on the basis of a large amount of material in English, arrived at a more or less empirical system with seven main mechanisms of semantic change which he then justified on psychological grounds. Professor Stephen Ullmann has produced a neater system, on a deductive and psychological basis, with a division into two main headings (Association between Senses, Association between Names) each with two sub-headings (Similarity, Contact): but in practice, when discussing particular cases, he also brings in a number of other concepts (euphemism, amelioration, etc.).

In considering examples of semantic change which I have noticed in Present-day English, I shall not try to fit them into any rigid system; I shall, however, try to illustrate some of the common types of semantic change. First, as a matter of interest, I shall give a historical example of one of Stern's mechanisms of semantic change, the one that he calls *permutation*; the example (discussed in detail by Stern himself) is the change in meaning of the word *bead*. Originally *bead* meant "prayer"; how did it come to have its present meaning "small ball"? The change arose from the practice in pre-Reformation England of counting one's prayers by means of a rosary. The phrase *to tell one's beads* meant "to count one's prayers": but in an actual situation, when somebody said "he's telling his beads," what the hearer would in fact see was a man moving the little balls on his rosary; it was thus possible for the hearer to misinterpret the phrase by taking *beads* to mean "balls on the rosary" (a meaning first found in the late fourteenth century). This is an example of what Stern calls *equivocation*; the word *beads* in this situation can be taken by the hearer to mean either "prayers" or "balls on the rosary," but it makes no real difference to his understanding of the phrase as a whole whether he analyses it one way or the other; it makes no difference, in Stern's phrase, to his "adequate apprehension of the phrase referent." Later, however, a person who has mis-apprehended *beads* in this way may use it in a different context in which the original meaning "prayer" is impossible; he may say, for example, that the beads on his rosary are made of ivory; and thus the new meaning is launched on its career.

Turning to Present-day English, we may first notice that some changes of meaning are due to changes in things rather than in words. For example, the word *house* (haus) has as one of its main meanings "a building designed and used as a human habitation," and it has had this meaning for hundreds of years; yet a modern house, with glass windows and a kitchen-sink and a bathroom and perhaps with central-heating and parquet flooring, is quite different from any house that existed in the middle ages; the dictionary-definition of a house has remained unchanged, but the objects in practice referred to by the word *house* have changed considerably. Similarly, there has in practice been a change of meaning in the words *ship*, *pistol*, *knife*, *coat*, *king*, *parliament*, and so on, as the objects or institu-tions denoted by these words have undergone a process of historical evolution. Again, we can say that *aeroplane* no longer has exactly the same meaning as it had fifty years ago, in the days of struts and canvas. Such changes of meaning have taken place even in the animal and vegetable kingdoms, thanks to selective breeding: medieval *sheep* and *horses* differed a great deal from the sheep and horses found on our farms to-day (the sheep were much longer-legged and the horses smaller), and the *rose* that Shakespeare wrote about was not much like the typical garden-rose in England to-day.

Similar changes have been undergone by many words in more abstract realms—words concerned with concepts, values, and so on. For example, the word *modest* has as one of its meanings, chiefly used of women, "chaste in behaviour, speech, bearing, dress, etc."; this meaning is an old-established one, but it is clear that the kind of behaviour which in practice is referred to as modest has changed a great deal in the past few hundred years, and even in our own lifetimes; a modern Englishwoman can wear clothes that would have seemed shockingly immodest a hundred years ago, she can discuss topics that were taboo for women in the Victorian age, she can do things that would have been unseemly in her grandmother's youth, and still not incur the charge of immodesty. Even more complicated are the changes that have taken place in the past few hundred years in concepts such as *nature*, *wit*, and *beauty*, and in scientific concepts such as *matter* and *atom*.

Such changes, however, though important for the historian of ideas, and indeed for every reader of the literature of the past, are not of very great interest to the linguist; the cases that interest him are not so much the ones where language is conservative and the universe changes, but rather the ones where language itself changes. Many such changes are going on in English to-day, and some of them are due in part to the existence in the English vocabulary of such a large number of "opaque" words. The existence of so many learned words derived from the classical languages has, throughout the Modern English period, led to frequent misuse and misunderstanding: Shakespeare's clowns and rustics constantly misuse long words ("Oh villain! thou will be condemned into everlasting redemption for this"); and Sheridan made such misuse the sole basis for a character in a play, Mrs Malaprop in *The Rivals*; it is surely significant that the word *malapropism*, derived from this character, should have become so firmly established in the English language: there was obviously a need for it. In our own times, the tendency to misuse learned words has been further encouraged by the decline of the classics in our educational system, which has made our vocabulary more opaque, and by the rise of universal education, which has brought millions of people into contact with words (in newspapers and books) which are unfamiliar in their home-environment. A mistake by a single speaker will not have any lasting effect on the language, but often the same mistake is committed by many speakers, because of some typical situation in which the word is commonly used, or perhaps because of something in the structure of the word itself, and then a semantic change is in process.

A recent example of a sense-change in an opaque word of this kind is the verb to *evacuate*. Before the War, this meant "to empty, remove the contents from" (e.g. the air from a glass tube), or, in military contexts, "to withdraw one's forces from." Shortly before the outbreak of the Second World War, the Government carried out a partial evacuation of London and other big cities as a precaution against air-raids: schoolchildren and many non-essential workers were sent out into the country. In the press and on the wireless there was of course much discussion of this process, and the words *evacuate* and *evacuation*, which had previously been unknown to many of the population, were used freely. The new meaning probably arose from usages involving the noun *evacuation*: the expression *the evacuation of London* was taken as meaning, not the *emptying of London*, but the *removal (of the population) from London*; this is another example of what Stern calls equivocation: the hearer understands the phrase perfectly well, but analyses it incorrectly. Then, *evacuation* having been apprehended as meaning "removal," the verb *evacuate* was used to mean "remove, transport away"; it was especially common in the passive, and people would often say "I've been evacuated from London," or quite simply "I've been evacuated"; this last usage caused much ribald comment from people who knew the word in its original sense (which was often medical, as in *to evacuate the bowels*), but the new meaning has persisted as the popular one. At the same period, the new noun *evacuee* was coined, meaning "person who has been removed into the country."

This change took place in a short space of time. Others take place slowly, with constant resistance from the schools, and often to the accompaniment of denunciatory letters in *The Times*. One which has been spreading slowly for many years is a change in the verb *aggravate*; from meaning "make worse, intensify the gravity of," this has come to mean "vex, exasperate, annoy": there has been a transfer from the process to people's feelings about it. The new meaning has in fact existed since the seventeenth century, but in the earlier part of this century it was certainly substandard; Fowler condemned it half a century ago, and until the Second World War it was still considered a vulgarism; since the War, however, it has spread widely, and is now well on the way to general acceptance. It is true that many middle-class people, when they use the word in this sense ("Isn't it *aggravating*"), put on a comic pseudo-Cockney voice, to show that really they know that this is not good usage: but this is a typical defence-mechanism—by being jocular, they are taking out an insurance against the purist; such semi-jocular usage is in fact a step towards acceptance.

Another example of such a change of meaning in a "hard word" is the verb to *substitute* (*for*) "to put in place (of)," which is nowadays quite often used in the sense "to replace (by)"; in this case, probably, people have known the noun *substitute* as a synonym of *replacement*, and have then apprehended the two verbs as synonyms. An example of a technical expression formed from native elements is the noun *watershed*, "elevation dividing two river-systems," which is now sometimes used to mean "river-basin" (a meaning recorded since the late nineteenth century); this is probably a case where a compound-word is more easily misunderstood because of changes which have taken place in the independent elements from which it was originally formed; the word *shed* originally meant "to divide, separate," and it is in this sense that it was used in the compound noun *watershed*; now, however, *shed* no longer has this meaning, and it is easy for a modern speaker to associate the -*shed* of *watershed* with vague ideas of pouring out, flowing, the falling of rain, etc., because of the modern meanings of the verb *to shed*. Other examples of changes of this kind can easily be found by looking in school composition-books designed for G.C.E. Ordinary Level, and seeing the mistakes that pupils are warned against; though of course not all such usages are destined to become accepted.

Some of the changes going on to-day seem to be caused by the form or structure of the word itself, especially when it resembles some other word with which it can be confused. An example of this is *disinterested*, which has the normal modern meaning of "impartial, not actuated by selfish motives." In the seventeenth century, it was also used to mean "uninterested, not interested," but this meaning died out. It arose again, however, in the nineteen-twenties, but for a long time was sub-standard: even fifteen years ago it was regarded as a schoolboy howler: but recently it has spread rapidly, and can now be found in highly reputable newspapers and periodicals; more-over, this usage has led to a revival of the noun *disinterest*, which was very nearly dead, in the sense "lack of interest." The modern use of *disinterested* to mean "uninterested" is probably an innovation, unconnected with the seventeenth-century usage, and is due quite simply to the resemblance between the two words *uninterested* and *disinterested*: both *un-* and *dis-* are prefixes which can have the force of negation, and it seems that the two words have been confused.

An example which I have not yet seen in print, but which is common in essays by university students, is the use of *enormity*, "extreme wickedness, outrageous crime," to mean "great size"; the confusion here is with *enormousness*. Probably it is a case of analogy, the pair *enormous/enormity* being made to conform semantically to the pattern of pairs like *capacious/capacity*, *sagacious/sagacity*. Other examples of pairs of similar words frequently confused with each other are *adopt/adapt*, and *sensuous/sensual*. Another example which is still to be classed as a "mistake" is the strange confusion between *ingenuous* ("frank, sincere, artless") and *disingenuous* ("insincere, not candid, dis-honest"), which I have several times seen in print in recent years. Since the War, *disingenuous* has become a fashionable euphemism among political journalists; to say that a politician's explanation is disingenuous is felt to be politer than to say that he's a liar. But several times in such contexts (including one in the first leader of a highly reputable newspaper) I have seen the word *ingenuous* used instead (when the context showed clearly that *disingenuous* was meant). This is puzzling, since the words have exactly opposite meanings. Perhaps, the word having become fashionable, it has been picked up by writers who have never used it before, and who are therefore liable to make mistakes with it; and perhaps the confusion has been encouraged by the fact that *ingenuous* too can be a pejorative word, especially in political contexts, with the implication of "naïve, foolishly simple."

A final example of these changes of meaning due to form is

provided by the pairs of words in *-ic* and *-ical*; in some of these pairs, differentiation of meaning has taken place; for example *economic* ("having to do with economics") against *economical* ("frugal, not wasteful"), and *historic* ("famous or important in history") against *historical* ("having to do with history"); in such cases, however, the distinction between the two is nowadays often confused, so that people use *historic* to mean "having to do with history," and *economic* to mean "frugal, not wasteful." The resemblances between members of such pairs, it seems, has led to confusion between them; at the same time analogy is at work, since there are some such pairs in which there is no marked differentiation of meaning (*comic/comical, botanic/botanical*). There is also a levelling tendency, the *-ic* forms in general tending to drive out the *-ical* forms. However, there are still a number of firmly differentiated pairs, like *politic* ('pɔlitik), "judicious," and *political* (pə'litikl), "having to do with politics"; though in this particular pair it will be seen that the two words are also differentiated by stressing.

Most of my examples so far have involved a change to what is in effect a totally unrelated meaning. One very common kind of semantic change, however, is a change in the width of a word's reference: the meaning is generalised from some narrow field to a wider one, or narrowed down to a special field from a more general one. A historical example of the narrowing or specialising process is seen in the verb to *starve*, which in Old English meant simply "to die," but which in the sixteenth century became specialised in the sense "to die of hunger." Similarly, the noun *meat* originally meant "food," but now refers only to one special type of food (a specialisation that took place in the fifteenth century); the earlier meaning still survives in set phrases like *meat and drink* and *one man's meat is another man's poison*. An example of the opposite process, extension of meaning, is seen in the word *junk*, "rubbish, useless stuff"; this was originally a sailor's word, meaning "old rope," but has been extended since the late nineteenth century to cover anything useless; it is a good example of the way in which a word may extend its meaning when it moves out of the language of a special group into more general currency. It is interesting that the expression *old rope* is also used to mean "rubbish, something

extension
of
meaning

worthless," in the phrase *it's money for old rope* ("it's a bargain, it's easy, it's a big return for little effort"). The word *rubbish* itself is an example of extension of meaning; in Middle English it meant "broken stones and building material, fragments of plaster," in other words what we to-day should call *rubble*, but its meaning has since been extended to cover anything useless or worthless.

A modern example of extension of meaning is seen in *alibi*; this word (from Latin *alibi*, "elsewhere") is a technical legal term, meaning "plea that the accused was somewhere else when the crime was committed, and therefore cannot be guilty of it." It has moved from its specialist sphere into general usage because of the popularity, in our time, of the detective-story. Here it still retains the idea of *place*, and is commonly used in the sense "evidence that a suspect was somewhere else when the crime was committed." Outside detective fiction, however, it has in recent years come to mean "evidence of innocence" or "plea of innocence," with no necessary implication of place, and even just "plausible excuse"; thus I once heard a man who had failed to attend an important meeting say afterwards "It's all right: I've got an alibi," meaning that he could produce a good reason or excuse for his absence; this example shows the change of meaning very clearly, since the speaker obviously did not mean that he could prove he was absent from the meeting.

Another sphere from which technical terms have been borrowed and extended in meaning is that of psychology, especially psychoanalysis; one example is *complex*, which to psychoanalysts means a group of ideas or desires which has been repressed, that is, thrust into the unconscious; but nowadays the word is popularly used to mean "fixed mental tendency" or "obsession," without either "group" or "repressed" playing any part in its meaning: people often say *I've got an inferiority complex*, meaning simply "I suffer from a sense of inferiority"; and when they say *I've got a complex about X* they often mean "I react in some unusual way to X" or "I have an emotional set-up that makes it impossible for me to do X" or even "I can't cope with X, I know I shall fail." Another psychological term that has broken loose in everyday speech is *sadism*; to the psychologist this word implies a sexual perversion:

a sadist is one who obtains sexual pleasure by maltreating others: but in popular usage it has been generalised to mean simply "cruelty," with no sexual implication.

Another word that has had a great vogue recently comes from the sphere of medicine: *allergic*. Originally, it seems, *allergy* was the phenomenon in which an organism, on being given the same stimulus twice with a time interval between, reacts differently on the two occasions (one of the reactions often being an extremely violent one). Recently the medical profession themselves seem to have generalised the meaning somewhat, and now use *allergy* to mean "(particular kind of) hypersensitivity to stimulus"; to be *allergic* to something, there- fore, means to react to it with unusual violence, as for example the hay-fever patient does to various kinds of pollen. Because of recent medical research into allergic conditions, some of which are of immediate concern to large numbers of people, the word has come into general circulation since the War; and it is now used of reactions of any kind against anything; *I'm allergic to eggs* often means "eggs disagree with me," or even merely "I don't like eggs"; in *I'm allergic to film-stars* (which I have heard), it means simply "I don't like film-stars." I have come across examples of this popular use of *allergic* in several recent books by literary scholars, both English and American.

Two final examples of modern extension: *gambit* and *lay-by*. A *gambit* is a chess-opening in which White offers a pawn- sacrifice, but in popular usage the word is used for the opening moves in any kind of transaction or negotiation, without any implication of sacrifice. The word *lay-by* (ˈleibai) was coined in the second half of the nineteenth century to denote the part of a river where barges are "laid by" out of use; in the early twentieth century it is found extended by analogy to mean "railway-siding"; and in the past few years has come into general use to denote the place where a motorist or lorry-driver can pull off the road to rest.

The opposite process, the narrowing of meaning, is seen in the present-day development of the verb to *discipline*; this verb, formed by conversion from the noun *discipline*, used to mean "provide discipline, train, control," but recently it has been specialised in the sense "to punish": one particular aspect of providing discipline has been singled out and made the whole meaning. There is as a matter of fact an old ecclesiastical meaning of the verb to *discipline*, "to scourge, chastise," but the modern meaning "to punish" has probably arisen independently of this. Another example is the verb to *refute*, "disprove, confute"; recently it has been specialised by some speakers to mean simply "deny, contradict, *assert* that an argument is false" (which is a very small part indeed of the process of disproving). The new meaning is now quite common in the press and in B.B.C. news bulletins, and for people who still use the word in its older sense it is rather shocking to hear on the B.B.C., which has a reputation for political impartiality, a news-report that Politician A has *refuted* the arguments of Politician B. This probably illustrates the kind of context in which the change of meaning has taken place, and is a reflexion on the standards of proof adopted in political argument: it suggests that many people must have heard speakers claim to have *refuted* (*disproved*) an argument when in fact they have done nothing more than *contradict* it.

A word that has undergone more than one specialisation in modern times is the noun *model*. In dressmaking, it has come to mean "article made by a recognised designer" (*latest Paris models*). In engineering, and especially in motor-car manufacture, it has come to mean "(car etc.) of a particular design" (*Road Tests of 1928 Models*). It has also become extremely common in the sense "woman who poses for a commercial photographer (especially for advertising)" and "woman who wears and exhibits to customers new costumes etc. in a shop": these two jobs are in fact often combined in one person. For the second of them, the word *mannequin* used to be common, but has now gone out of use. From the noun *model* in this sense has been formed the new intransitive verb *to model*, "work as a model, act as a mannequin" (as in *she models for Dior*). The older meanings of *model*, both as noun and as verb, continue unchanged, but to many people (especially adolescent girls) the new meaning is the normal one, because fashion-modelling has been built up by the post-war mass-media as the ideal career for the teen-age girl (or rather as the first stage of a career which will continue via a Hollywood contract to a marriage with a millionaire). Rather similar as a social phenomenon is the specialisation of the word *photogenic*; this began as a technical term meaning "suitable for being photographed"; however, one aspect of this suitability has been seized on, namely sex-appeal, and now the word is commonly used to mean "good-looking, glamorous."

A recent example of a word that has been generalised and then specialised again in a different sense is the noun *probe*. Until recently this was only a medical word (dating from the sixteenth century) meaning "instrument for exploring a wound." The verb (dating from the seventeenth century) meant "to explore a wound with a probe," but also had the more general meaning "to examine thoroughly, investigate." In our own day, the noun too has been similarly generalised to mean "investigation, examination"; this has no doubt happened on analogy with the verb, but the dissemination of the new meaning has been encouraged by the press, which has found the noun *probe* a useful short word for headlines, meaning "investigation" (*Labour Demands Rent Probe.*, *i.e.*, "the Labour Party demands an investigation of rents"). Recently, however, *probe* has been specialised again to mean "space vehicle for scientific investigation" (for *probing space*, as they say), and there are even signs of its being used to mean simply "space vehicle," which would be an interesting development. This is not merely a popular or newspaper usage, but is also heard on the lips of eminent scientists.

We can also consider as a form of specialisation the process by which a word acquires implications of desirability or undesirability; a historical example of this is the word *lust*, which originally meant "pleasure, delight, desire," but later came to be a pejorative word meaning "lascivious desire"; here there has been a double specialisation, for the meaning has been narrowed to specifically sexual desire, and at the same time an implication of excess or illicitness has been introduced; the related verb to *list* (now obsolete), meaning "to be pleasing, to take pleasure in, to desire" (*The wind bloweth where it listeth*) escaped this specialisation. In our own day there are similar examples of words acquiring unfavourable implications. One is *appeasement*, which means "process of appeasing, assuaging,"

but which has acquired a pejorative sense in political contexts
(implying an undesirable policy of conciliation towards an
aggressive power) because of the pre-war policies of Mr Neville
Chamberlain towards Hitler, and their outcome. Other political words have been similarly affected by events, sometimes
only temporarily, for example *collaborator*. Sometimes the
process of specialisation is in the opposite direction, and
favourable implications are acquired: the word *success* originally
meant simply "result," but as early as the sixteenth century
came to mean "good result." An example from the political
sphere is the word *democratic*, which during the past couple of
centuries has changed from being a neutral word, and indeed
often a pejorative one, to being one of the key-concepts of the
Western way of life. It is also possible for words to lose their
favourable or unfavourable implications, and become morally
neutral; the word *politician* (while still not exactly a term of
praise) has lost the implications of villainy and deceit that it
had in Shakespeare's day: and the word *woman*, which to many
people thirty or forty years ago sounded faintly disreputable,
has become fully respectable again, so that genteelisms like
lady-teacher and *charlady* are no longer felt necessary and indeed
sound rather comic.

Not all changes of meaning, however, are examples of
specialisation or extension; the changes we have noticed in
bead, *evacuate*, and *disinterested* are not of this kind; here we
rather have a transfer to a quite different meaning. In these
three cases, the transfer is plainly unintentional; and there are
many more of this type. Thus the word *chronic*, meaning
"lasting for a long time," is now frequently used to mean "bad,
irreclaimable, incurable"; the change is plainly due to the
common use of *chronic* of diseases, for people tend to think that a
chronic disease must be a serious one (though in fact for a
doctor *chronic* and *acute* are terms of contrast). Another unintentional transfer is the use of the word *book* to mean "magazine";
in some circles, indeed, there is a tendency for a *book* to be
specialised to mean "novel," simply because the novel is the
main literary form of our age: but if you ask a class of girls in a
secondary-modern school what books are read in their homes
they will give you a list of things like *Woman's Own* and *Every-*

body's; this transfer is presumably due to the fact that, apart from newspapers, magazines are the only kind of reading-matter available in their homes; this is an alarming cultural symptom, and it is to be hoped that the new meaning will not become widely disseminated. Perhaps we can also reckon as unintentional the transfer in the word *atomic* ("having to do with atoms"); first it has developed a meaning "having to do with nuclear fission," shading off into "using the energy derived from nuclear fission," and "characterised by the use of such energy": *atomic pile, atomic power-station, this atomic age*. Then, because it has become associated in the popular mind with great power and with up-to-dateness, it has come to be used to mean "very big," as in *an atomic effort*, or as a rather vague prestige-word, as in *an atomic blonde* (presumably one whose effect on men is comparable in devastation to that of an atom-bomb). Rather similar is the slangy use of *supersonic* in the sense of "super, very good," which is heard occasionally.

Recently I have noticed what may be the beginnings of a couple of unintentional transfers in the sphere of shopping and advertising. The first is the tendency of *economy* used as a noun-adjunct to develop the meaning "large"; a manufacturer who sells some product in packages of more than one size often calls attention to the fact that it is cheaper to buy the largest-sized packet, because you get proportionately more for your money; hence the largest packet is frequently called "economy size"; from this it is a very short step to "economy packet," a description which is, for example, common for the largest-sized packet of many breakfast cereals; it is quite likely, therefore, that many people are already apprehending *economy* to mean "large." Rather similar is the incipient development in the word *budget*, except that this is confined to goods that are specifically feminine; women's magazines have a habit of drawing up ideal weekly or monthly budgets for the housewife, to show how to save money and yet have all the things you want; in order to get things both ways like this, the compilers of such budgets have to find things that are cheap, and this often means *small*; consequently a *budget item* is coming to be apprehended by women as something that is cheap or something in a small-sized packet; and I have in fact seen in shop-windows small-sized packets of cosmetics labelled "budget size"; so perhaps *budget* is beginning to develop the meaning "small." The decisive step, of course, would be the use of *economy* to mean "large" or *budget* to mean "small" in a different kind of context; if people started talking about *economy bundles of laundry* or *budget motor-cars*, then the new meaning really would have arrived: but this has not happened, and of course very likely never will happen. These changes are further examples of what Stern calls "permutation."

Many transfers of meaning, however, are not unintentional, but quite conscious. This is especially true of the change of meaning by figurative use of a word; the first person to talk about the *foot* of a hill, or to say that he *grasped* a meaning, must have been using a conscious metaphor; the new meaning has been used so many times since that it is no longer apprehended as figurative at all, and of course the language is full of such dead metaphors. Such a change of meaning is not a slow process, as many unintentional transfers are, but takes place with a single leap of the imagination; though of course the *dissemination* of the new meaning may be slow.

As at other times, the language to-day is full of new figurative usages, some of which are rapidly ceasing to be felt as figurative at all. Nowadays, a difficult problem is a *headache*; we have *blanket* legislation to cover the whole of an issue; we try to avoid *bottlenecks* in order to increase our *global* ("total") production and to achieve our *targets*, while assiduously protecting our national *lifelines* and arguing about *ceilings* for wages and prices, which some people would like to *freeze* at their present levels and others not. The word *target* illustrates the speed with which a new figurative meaning can cease to be felt as figurative; the meaning "output aimed at in a given period" has not been in common use for very many years, but people do not talk about *hitting* or *missing* such targets: instead we *achieve* our targets, or *fulfil* them or *overfulfil* them, or *reach* them, or even *overshoot* them; to anybody who is still conscious of *target* as a metaphor, such usages are ludicrous, but this of course is only a transitional phase: the metaphor will become a dead one for everybody within quite a short time.

A sphere that has naturally called for a large number of

new words or new meanings in the present century is that of aeronautics, and here too a good deal has been done by the figurative use of existing words. Even when we say that an aircraft *climbs* or *dives* we are using a (dead) metaphor; and an aircraft, too, has a *ceiling*. When a fighter pilot flies at the rear of a formation and zigzags back and forth to protect the formation from the rear, he is said to *weave* (intransitive); the image here is from the thread going back and forth in cloth, or the shuttle of the handloom going under and over the warp. When the formation carries out a *sweep* over enemy territory, the image is a domestic one, that of a broom; and when it provides an *umbrella* for troops or ships, its imagery reflects the climate and habits of the speakers. Quite a few aeronautical terms are borrowed from seafaring: *pilot*, the *towing* of gliders by a *tug* (aircraft), *port* and *starboard*, the *feathering* of an airscrew (from the feathering of an oar), and so on. It may be felt that some of these are so obvious that they are to be thought of as slight extensions of width of meaning, rather than as figurative transfers: but perhaps they are only obvious because we are used to them; we do not, it should be noticed, talk about the port and starboard sides of a train or of a car, and if anybody did so we should surely feel that his language was figurative.

Another kind of semantic change which is common in all periods is *loss of intensity*, the weakening of meaning which occurs because of the very human tendency to exaggerate, or to simulate a feeling that does not exist. This kind of fading can be seen in the word *awful*, which used to mean "inspiring awe and reverence," but because of constant exaggeration has now come to mean merely "unpleasant" (*I've had an awful day at the office*), or even to be used simply as an intensifier meaning something like "large, great" (*I've got an awful lot of work to do*). In the adverb *awfully* the fading is even more marked, and it means little more than "very" (*I'm awfully glad you were able to come*). Similar loss of intensity is being undergone by *dreadful*, *appalling*, *frightful*, and other such words used to evoke powerful emotions. Among speech-groups that like to be up-to-the-minute there is a frequent demand for new intensive words of vague meaning, as the old ones get worn out, and the last few decades have seen the rise and fall of many such words as *ghastly, frightful, hideous, sickmaking,* and so on, and on the positive side *smashing, shattering, wizard, bang-on, super, super-duper, massive, fabulous,* and so on. There are phase-differences between different speech-groups, and it would be unsafe to assume that the words currently fashionable in a Birmingham rock-and-roll club were simultaneously fashionable in a West End night-club, or that the picturesque phrases used by schoolboys were still fashionable in R.A.F. messes.

Another kind of word especially subject to fading is that connected with punctuality; we have already noticed the fate of *presently,* which used to mean "immediately"; but it looks as though *immediately* may itself be going the same way; we all know that, when we call for an acquaintance and he says that he will be ready *immediately,* we may well have to wait ten minutes; and *at once* seems little better. Some people seem to use *this moment* or *this very moment* when they wish to indicate real immediacy, and these may be phrases with a future.

Another cause of semantic change which is found in all periods is the coining of *euphemisms.* Topics which are unpleasant to think about, like death and war and disease, or which are subject to social taboos, like sex and defecation, tend to be softened or skirted round by the use of near-synonyms or indirect expressions. However, a euphemism soon wears out, for after a time it is no longer felt as a euphemism, but simply as the word for the thing in question, and a new euphemism has to be found; and so the process of change of meaning goes on. We are perhaps not as much addicted to euphemism as our Victorian ancestors (who thought it indelicate to talk about the *legs* of a piano), but the habit is nevertheless deep-rooted. Death is one of the topics that people feel it is indelicate to mention too directly, and we have a large number of euphemisms for it; one of the common ones which seems to have arisen in our time is the expression of the type *If anything should happen to me* ("If I should die"); this is frequently used, for example, in advertisements by insurance-companies. Wartime slang in the armed forces was full of euphemisms for being killed (*he's had it, he's bought it, he's gone for a Burton, he's had his time, he's handed in his chips,* etc. etc.).

In post-war politics, it is war and economic collapse that have

especially evoked euphemism; *military* expenditure, it goes
without saying, is always *defence* expenditure; the word *war*
itself is felt to be indelicate, and official literature instead talks
about an *emergency*; small wars are *local operations* or *local hostilities*
and the *hydrogen-bomb* is the *deterrent*. Before the War, the great
economic collapse of the early nineteen-thirties was called the
Slump; soon, however, this came to be felt as a smear-word, and
was replaced in official circles by the politer word *Depression*;
after the War, whenever there was any discussion of the
possibility of a trade-depression, this word itself was now felt
to be too blunt, and was replaced by *recession*; now this in turn
is being threatened by *downturn*; this word was used in a speech
by Mr Harold Wilson in April 1960, and he felt it necessary
to add the gloss "This is economist's language for what the
common man calls a recession"; no doubt this word too will
gradually spread to the language of "the common man."

In the field of social taboos, it is lavatories that especially
cause euphemism to proliferate; it must be difficult for the
foreigner visiting England to keep track of the many variants
(*lavatory, toilet, cloak-room, gentlemen, gents, ladies' room, ladies,
W.C., the bathroom*), not to mention the innumerable phrases
(*to wash one's hands, spend a penny,* etc.). The upper-class word
seems to be *lavatory*; among other classes, however, the word
toilet is very widely used, and may be going up in the world;
it is used, for example, on B.E.A. and B.O.A.C. airliners, where
it comes up in coloured lights, though the stewardesses often
use instead the word *washroom*. The other great field of taboo
is sex, and there are innumerable euphemisms clustered around
the subject. New words are constantly having to be found, for
example, to describe a woman of doubtful virtue (to use an
old-fashioned euphemism), and there is a constant danger that
innocent expressions like *sweetheart* and *girl-friend* will become
pejorative.

Since the spread of democratic sentiments in our community, people have also found it indelicate or politically
inexpedient to mention too bluntly the differences between
individuals—differences of endowment, of possessions, of social
class. Euphemisms are found, for example, for people who are
below the average intellectually: in popular speech there are

many words like *dim* and *dim-witted* ("stupid"), and in official
language there is the expression *mentally deficient* (which of course
has an exact meaning in terms of I.Q.), which is further
softened by the use of initials to *m.d.*; another example of
initials as a euphemism is *e.s.n.*, used in schools to mean
"educationally sub-normal" (itself a charming euphemism).
As for *class*, this is often described in terms of *education*: a man
of the lower classes is described as an *uneducated man*; words
suggesting "niceness" as opposed to "roughness" are also often
used: a middle-class residential area is a *nice* district. Moreover,
nowadays we are no longer rich or poor: instead we are placed
in a higher or a lower *income-bracket*, and the poor and oppressed
of the world have become the *underprivileged*.

It is often asserted that euphemism is especially characteristic of the middle classes, and that the upper classes avoid it.
It is possible that the middle classes, being in the Puritan
tradition, have a slightly greater tendency to use euphemisms,
but this should not be exaggerated. The upper-class word
lavatory is just as much a euphemism as the middle-class word
toilet; the upper-class speaker may not feel the word *lavatory* as a
euphemism, but the same is true of the middle-class speaker
with the word *toilet*. In fact we tend to notice other people's
euphemisms more than our own. The same is true of "genteelisms"; upper-class writers often speak with great scorn of
such lower-middle-class usages as *dessert* ("pudding"), *serviette*
("table-napkin"), *mirror* ("looking-glass") and *stomach* ("belly"),
which are condemned as pretentious euphemisms used by
people for whom the simple everyday word is not good enough.
But this of course is absurd. Whatever the origins of these
usages may have been, they are now, for millions of people who
use them, the ordinary everyday word they have learnt in their
home environment; for such people, it would be pretentious to
use the upper-class *table-napkin*, etc.: in their speech environment, it is these that would be the genteelisms.

One final source of new meanings may be mentioned: the
newspapers. Quite apart from their role in the dissemination
of new words and new meanings, they actually create new
meanings, especially by their habit of choosing the short and
snappy word for the headline; this word may not mean exactly

what they want to say, but, like Humpty-Dumpty in *Alice Through the Looking-Glass*, they make it mean what they want it to mean. We have already noticed the word *probe*, used by the press in the sense "investigation." Other examples, among many, are the verb to *rap*, used to mean "to rebuke," and the noun *bid*, used to mean "attempt." It may be thought that these new meanings are confined to the newspapers, and do not get into ordinary speech; there is some sign, however, that this may be happening: words of this kind are now frequently used in their newspaper-meanings by journalists broadcasting on sound-radio or on television, and this increases greatly the likelihood of their being taken into everyday speech.

Chapter V:

Notes and suggestions for further reading

The pioneer modern work on semantics was Michel Bréal's *Essai de sémantique* (Paris 1921). Gustaf Stern's book on semantic change in English is *Meaning and Change of Meaning* (Gothenburg 1931). A comprehensive survey of the whole field will be found in Professor Stephen Ullmann's book *The Principles of Semantics* (2nd edn., Glasgow 1957); an easier book for beginners is the same author's more popular work, *Words and their Use* (London 1951). It should be noted that I do not use the word *transfer* in the special technical sense given it by Stern; it is the name of one of his seven types of sense-change, but I use it in a general sense.

The semantic histories of individual English words can be studied, within limits, in the *N.E.D.*, though it is often risky to draw conclusions about the processes of semantic change from the dictionary alone. Specialist studies on semantic developments in small groups of related English words include Gustaf Stern, *Swift, Swiftly and their Synonyms* (Gothenburg 1921); Arne Rudskoger, *Fair, Foul, Nice, Proper: a Contribution to the Study of Polysemy* (Stockholm 1952); and Svante Stubelius, *Airship, Aeroplane, Aircraft: Studies in the History of Terms for Aircraft in English* (Gothenburg 1958). In my own work, *The Idea of Honour in the English Drama 1591-1700* (Gothenburg 1957), I have tried to use the semantic development of one word as a key to cultural and social history.

A book that has had a great influence is *The Meaning of Meaning*, by C. K. Ogden and I. A. Richards (London 1923). Richards's ideas have been developed and modified by William Empson, who

Chapter VI

Grammatical Changes

To know a language, it is not sufficient to know the words: you must also know how to combine them into groups to form meaningful utterances. That is, you must know the *grammar* of the language. It is customary to divide grammar into two main parts, *morphology* and *syntax* (though some writers use the word *grammar* in a narrower sense to refer to what I call *morphology*). Morphology deals with the structure of the single word, for example with the way the form of a word changes in different syntactic situations (*man/man's/men/men's* or *walk/walks/walking/walked*); parts of Chapter IV, for example on the way words are constructed from affixes and roots, are also within the field of morphology, but in the present chapter I shall touch on morphology only insofar as it bears directly on syntax, which in practice means inflexional morphology. Syntax deals with the structure of *groups* of words: the ways in which the words of the language can combine into groups, and in which these groups can combine with each other. The syntax of modern English is extremely complicated; if you doubt this, examine your own usage and try to give a systematic account of such things as the definite article (when do you use it, and when not?), the position of the adverb in the sentence, the use of *some* and *any* (when do you use which?), the use of the present continuous tense (*e.g.*, *I am working*), and so on. (If you are not a native speaker of English, you will hardly need evidence of the complication.) Fortunately, we do not need any such conscious systematic knowledge of syntax in order to be able to use the language: we have learnt to observe the conventions governing English without formulating them, by a long process of listening and practice in our childhood (children work very hard learning their mother-tongue), so that now it comes as naturally to us as breathing.

Like the phonology and the vocabulary, the grammar of a language is subject to change, as we have already noticed in Chapter I. During the last thousand years and more, there have been many changes in English grammar, but there is one broad trend that stands out clearly: the language has come to rely less and less on a system of word-inflexions, and more and more on word-order and on function-words (*e.g.*, prepositions, auxiliary verbs); English has become less *synthetic* and more *analytic*. Inflexions still play an important part in English, but there are very few of them compared with the great inflexional system of Old English, which was comparable to that of modern German or of classical Latin. In Old English, prepositions played a much smaller part than they do in Modern English, much of their work being done by word-inflexions; and, although there were conventions governing word-order, this was much less crucial than in Modern English, and in Old English poetry there is a freedom of word-order rather like that in classical Latin poetry. The importance of word-order rather than word-inflexion in Modern English is made clear by a comparison with Latin: however much we change the word-order of *mens regit corpus* ("the mind governs the body"), we cannot make it mean "the body governs the mind" or "the body the mind governs" or "the mind the body governs"; but the English words, according to their arrangement, give four totally different meanings (two of them complete sentences, the other two just nouns modified by an adjective clause).

The inflexions that remain in English, however, mostly show little sign of erosion at the moment: the third person singular inflexion of the verb (he walk*s*), the past-simple inflexion (he walk*ed*), the -*ing* form (*walking*), the plural and possessive forms of the noun (*boy, boys, boy's, boys'*), the nominative-accusative contrast in the personal pronouns (*we/us, he/him*)—these things still seem as firm as rocks.

There are, however, a few signs that the process of loss of inflexions is still going on. It is especially clear in the contrast *who/whom*: the inflected form *whom* is disappearing from the spoken language and being replaced by *who*, though it still persists strongly in writing. It is entirely natural, for example, to say *I don't know who to suggest*, though many people would write *whom*. There is one position where *whom* is always used still, and that is immediately after a preposition which governs it: we cannot replace *whom* by *who* in the sentences *To whom shall I give it?* and *I don't know for whom it is intended*: but these sentences really belong to the written language, and sound extremely stilted in speech; most people in fact would say *Who shall I give it to?* and *I don't know who it's intended for*. It is also to be noted that *me* is now normally accepted as the form to use after the verb *to be* (like French *moi*); nowadays it sounds merely pedantic to say *It is I*, and the normal form is *It's me*. It is perhaps also significant that people often make "mistakes" with the contrasted forms of the personal pronouns; one frequently hears sentences like *he gave it to my brother and I* (where the pronoun is separated from the governing preposition by a noun); and there is a good deal of confusion about the case to be used after *but*, *as* and *like* (*nobody but me* or *nobody but I?*); these may be the first signs of an ultimate erosion of the nominative-accusative contrast in the personal pronouns, like that now taking place with *who*.

The continued loss of inflexions, and their replacement by syntactic devices, is also seen in the comparative and superlative of adjectives, where forms with *-er* and *-est* are being replaced by forms with *more* and *most*. Here we see the continuation of a trend of long standing: Milton wrote *elegantest*, *famousest*, and *sheepishest*, and Archbishop Laud *notoriousest*, where we should write *most elegant*, and so on. To-day, adjectives with three or more syllables are normally compared with *more* and *most* (*beautiful, more beautiful, most beautiful*); monosyllabic adjectives, on the other hand, are normally compared with *-er* and *-est* (*bright, brighter, brightest*). The adjectives with two syllables are divided, some usually being compared one way, the others the other; and it is in this dissyllabic group that the change is most noticeable, adjectives formerly taking *-er* and *-est* tending to go over to *more* and *most*. A word where this is especially noticeable is *common*; twenty or thirty years ago, *commoner* and *commonest* were normal, but nowadays nearly everybody says *more common, most common*. Indeed, I recently borrowed from a university library a book written in the nineteen-thirties by a distinguished literary scholar: in one place, the word *commonest* occurred; this had been vigorously crossed out by some borrower (presumably a student), who had written in the margin "most common!!!" Another example is heard in B.B.C. weather-forecasts, which frequently say that it will be *more cloudy*, instead of *cloudier*. Other adjectives that I have heard with *more* or *most* include *fussy*, *quiet*, *cruel*, *subtle*, *clever*, *profound*, *simple*, and *pleasant*; all these, I think, were normally compared with *-er* and *-est* before the War. I have also been struck by the frequency of forms like *more well-informed* and *most well-dressed*, where people would formerly have said *better-informed* and *best-dressed*. Recently there have been many cases of *more* and *most* spreading even to monosyllabic adjectives; examples I have noticed in educated speech and writing include *more crude*, *more plain*, and *more keen*. In Miss Iris Murdoch's well-known novel, *The Bell*, occurs the remarkable phrase *one of the most good people that he knew*.

On the other hand, there are one or two changes going on in the language which run counter to this trend towards loss or simplification of inflexions. One clear one is the spreading of the *'s*-genitive at the expense of the *of*-genitive. Until a few years ago, the genitive with *'s* was used in modern times mainly with nouns which could be replaced (in the singular) by the pronouns *he* and *she*, but not with nouns which could be replaced by the pronoun *it*: so that people normally said *the man's face* and *the woman's face*, but *the face of the clock* and *the surface of the water*. Actually, things were slightly more complicated than this: the *'s*-genitive was used in certain expression of time and distance (*an hour's sleep*), and could be used with many nouns replaceable in the singular by *it* or *they* (*the Government's decision*); there were also a number of commonly-used phrases where the *'s*-genitive was used even though the noun was one which could be replaced in the singular only by *it* (*New Year's Day*, *the water's edge*). In recent years, however, the *'s*-genitive has come into common use with nouns which are replaceable in the singular only by *it*. I will give a few examples that I have come across recently in my reading. A preface written by two university teachers of English speaks of *biography's charm*; an eminent archaeologist, writing about the archaeological record, uses the expression *the record's imperfection*; a well-known novelist, writing in a critical quarterly, talks of *evil's power*; the *Radio Times*, as the subtitle of a programme, gives *a study of the Congo's collapse*; a periodical published by a consumer's association puts *Resorts' Weather* as the title of an article on the weather of seaside towns; and a literary critic says that *criticism's standard is that of a reasonable man*. Other examples, all from reputable sources, include *human nature's diversity, Senate's committee, the beauty of Killarney's Lakes, the concern with virginity's preservation*, and *amendments to the game's laws* (of Rugby football). In all these, one would have expected *of*-forms unless the writer were deliberately using a personification. You will easily find many more examples in books and in the newspapers. It will be seen that this tendency for *'s* to replace *of* is a movement from the analytic to the synthetic: a syntactical phrase is being replaced by an inflexion.

Another surprising reversion which has taken place during the last twenty years is the partial revival of specifically sub-junctive forms of verbs. The subjunctive mood was used ex-tensively in Old English, as in classical Latin and modern German; since the Middle English period, however, it has been slowly dying out, its place being taken by compound verb-forms with auxiliaries (*should, might*, etc.). The only really firmly established subjunctive form surviving in English in the nineteen-thirties was *were*; it was (and still is) normal for an educated speaker to use *were* and not *was* in a "closed conditional clause," as in *If he were here, we should certainly be able to see him* (he is not here). There were other subjunctive survivals in sporadic use (as in *if it be so*), but these all sounded a trifle literary and affected. During and after the War, however, subjunctive forms increased in frequency, especially in the written language; this seems to have begun in the language of administration, and spread from there to the literary language. The forms used are third-person singular ones without in-flexion, as in *I insist that he do it, it was essential that he make a choice* (where *do* is used instead of *does* or *shall do*, and *make* instead of *should make*). Sentences of this type (especially the first) are also sometimes heard in speech. It is extremely unlikely, however, that we are going to see any serious long-term revival of the subjunctive forms; the present development is probably only a passing fashion. If it has any long-term significance, this is likely to be, not a revival of the subjunctive, but an eroding away of the third-singular inflexion; by accustoming people to forms like *he do* and *he make*, these usages may prepare the way for the ultimate disappearance of *he does* and *he makes*. This after all would be the natural continuation of the historical process; in the present-simple, we have lost all inflexions except the third-singular -*s*, and it would be quite natural to expect the process to continue, so that we had only one form all through the tense (*I walk, you walk, he walk, we walk, they walk*). This is more or less what has happened in Danish and (in the spoken language) in Swedish, though in these languages the single form preserved is in fact an inflected one. It may happen one day in English; though of course we can only guess.

Of the other changes going on, several have to do with auxiliary verbs. For example, the distinctions formerly made between *shall* and *will* are being lost, and *will* is coming increasingly to be used instead of *shall*. One reason for this is that in speech we very often say neither wil nor ʃæl, but just l: *I'll see you to-morrow, we'll meet you at the station, John'll get it for you.* We cannot use this weak form in all positions (not at the end of a phrase, for example), but we use it very often; and, whatever its historical origin may have been (probably from *will*), we now use it indiscriminately as a weak form for either *shall* or *will*; and very often the speaker could not tell you which he had intended. There is thus often a doubt in a speaker's mind whether *will* or *shall* is the appropriate form; and, in this doubt, it is *will* that is spreading at the expense of *shall*, presumably because *will* is used more frequently than *shall* anyway, and so is likely to be the winner in a levelling process. So people nowadays commonly say or write *I will be there, we will all die one day*, and so on, when they intend to express simple futurity and not volition. This has taken some of the edge off the old joke about the man who fell into a pond and cried out *I will be drowned, no one shall save me*; the first half of this no longer works as a joke, because many people take *I will be drowned* to express simple futurity; the second half, however, does still work, at any rate in British English, for *no one shall save me* must be taken as an expression of volition ("I refuse to be saved"), and this usage is still common. Another construction where *shall* still cannot be replaced by *will* is the type *I insist that he shall do it*: but in fact people tend increasingly to say *I insist that he do it* or *I insist that he does it*. The situation is much the same with *should* and *would*; there are still many contexts where *should* cannot be replaced by *would* (*I insisted that he should do it*), but people increasingly use *I would* and *we would* in contexts where previously *should* was normal (*I would like to know*; *if we were to tell you, we would be committing breach of faith*). As with *shall* and *will*, the process is probably helped by the use in speech of the same weak form, d, to replace both *should* and *would* (*I'd like to know, we'd be committing*).

Other changes are taking place among the auxiliary-verbs, and new auxiliaries are gaining ground. Mossé calls attention to the use of *get* and *want* as auxiliaries; *get* is used for forming a passive, as *he got hurt* and *you'll get hurt* (not new usages, but ones which are spreading); *want* is used to mean "ought" or "must" or "need," as in *you want to be careful what you're doing, you want to go to a doctor*, and *you want to take it easy*. It is also very common to use *get* followed by an *-ing*-form to mean "begin" (*let's get going*), and followed by a *to*-infinitive to indicate achievement (*I got to know him*); and forms like *I've got to* are used to indicate obligation or compulsion. Another auxiliary which is becoming extremely important is *be going* followed by a *to*-infinitive: this sometimes denotes intention (*I'm going to write another book*) and sometimes simple futurity (*he's going to be in trouble*). In most of these usages, the auxiliary is followed by a *to*-infinitive, and so differs from most of the traditional auxiliaries (*can, should, might*, etc.). Admittedly, the traditional auxiliaries *ought* and *used* are followed by a *to*-infinitive: but *ought* and *used*, like the other traditional auxiliaries, form their negative and interrogative without *do*, whereas *get* and *want* use *do*-forms (*you don't want to be rash, did you get to know him?*); so there are formal differences between the new auxiliaries and the old.

In the auxiliaries which are followed by a *to*-infinitive, there is a tendency for the *to* to become attached to the auxiliary, instead of to the following infinitive, so that *you ought to go* becomes ju(ː) ˈɔːtə ˈgou; it looks as though we are on the way to getting a new auxiliary *oughter*. Similarly, *want to go* tends to become wɔntə ˈgou, and in substandard speech ˈwɔnə ˈgou; and *I'm going to go* is often aim ˈgountə ˈgou in familiar speech, and ai ˈgɔnə ˈgou in substandard speech. This development seems to have gone farther in the United States than in Britain, and American fiction-writers writing dialogue often use the forms *oughta, wanna, gotta,* and *gonna*; indeed, I have met American teachers of English as a foreign language who teach their pupils that the future tense of the verb *to go* is *I gonna* (ˈgʌnə) *go, you gonna go,* etc. We have certainly not reached this stage yet in Britain, but it may very well come. Another construction that may well ultimately be assimilated to the *gonna* type is *had better*; this is frequently used with the *had* in a weak form, for example *you'd better wait* (jud ˈbetə ˈweit); in substandard speech, this often becomes (ju ˈbetə ˈweit). It is obvious that *better* (ˈbetə) may be interpreted as analogical with *ought to* (ˈɔːtə); and children, indeed, often say such things as *I'd better wait, betn't I?* (aid ˈbetə ˈweit ˈbetnt ai). I have never heard this in adult speech; it is still just an amusing childish error: but it may be a straw in the wind.

Another development that is mainly heard in children's speech, but which is now also heard occasionally in substandard adult speech, is the inverse form *of* for *have*; this has arisen because both *of* and *have* possess the weak form əv, as in *lots of money* (ˈlɔts əv ˈmʌni) and *I'd have done it* (ˈaid əv ˈdʌnit). The speaker then interprets the əv in the second of these as the weak form of *of*, and writes *I'd of done it*; he may even pronounce *have* as *of* (ɔv), especially in such sentences as *I'd have done it, wouldn't you have?* (ˈaid əv ˈdʌnit wudənt ˈjuː ˈɔv). This process is called *inversion*, and the spelling *of* (for *have*) is an inverse spelling.

While new auxiliaries are spreading, some of the older auxiliaries are disappearing in some positions. One is *have* when it is weakly stressed. The weak form is often just v, as in *we've done it* (wiːv ˈdʌnit). In substandard speech this v often disappears, and we get forms like *we done it, they been,* and *you seen* (though in some dialects these forms may have a different origin). Here then we have new forms of the present-perfect tense; they are still very definitely substandard in Britain, but may have a future. Another example is *do*, which often disappears in questions, especially second-person ones like *What you want that for?* and *Where you think you're going?*. This is still considered "careless," and does not appear in writing (except in dialogue), but it is quite common in speech, even educated speech. The words *does* and *did* do not disappear in this way, but are often replaced by new weak forms s and d, as in *What's he say?* (ˈwɔts hi ˈsei) and *Where'd you find that?* (ˈwɛədjə faind ˈðæt).

In second-person questions not introduced by an interrogative-word, other forms are often lost in familiar speech besides *do*. People often say *Like a cigarette?*, and *Have a drink?*, and (when telling someone the way) *See those traffic-lights?*. The second of these looks somewhat like an imperative, but is in fact distinguished from an imperative by its intonation: in the imperative, the pitch of the voice falls on *drink*, but in the interrogative it rises. The other two examples could hardly be taken as imperatives, even in print. What has in fact happened, plainly, is that words have dropped out (*Would you, Will you, Do you*). This particular ellipsis is only heard with the second person (*you*), but there it is extremely common, and in effect a new interrogative structure is developing for the second-person forms of verbs.

Changes are also taking place in the use of adverbs, prepositions, and conjunctions. A very obvious one is the use of *like* as a conjunction (as in *he can't do it like I can*); this has been attacked by purists for many years, and before the War it was still regarded as an illiterate usage, but since the War it has become very common; its spread has no doubt been encouraged by American example; to many people it is still extremely offensive, but it will hardly be stopped now. The phrase *same as* is also coming to be used as a conjunction, meaning "as, just as," for example *he likes football, same as I do*; this too used to be a vulgarism, but is now spreading in educated speech. Another usage no doubt encouraged by American practice is *due to* used as a preposition, another shibboleth of the purists; in old-fashioned speech, *due* may be followed by *to*, but must

be an adjective, as in *The money was due to him* and *His death was
due to heart-failure*; but from the second type, where *due to* is
equivalent to *caused by*, *owing to*, or *because of*, there has developed
a usage of the type *Due to heart-failure, he died*, where *due to* is a
compound preposition. An equivocal case can be seen in *He
suffered an early death, due to heart-failure*; the purist could accept
this, interpreting *due to heart-failure* as an adjective-phrase
modifying *death* (equivalent to *which was due to heart-failure*):
but the average reader nowadays would take it as an adverb
phrase of cause, modifying the whole sentence (equivalent to
because of heart-failure), which would then be identical in meaning with *Due to heart-failure, he suffered an early death*. It was
probably from such potentially equivocal constructions that the
new usage arose. It is still combated by the schools, but has
spread greatly since the War, is heard in B.B.C. news-bulletins,
and is well on the way to respectability.

The phrases *sort of* and *kind of* are coming to be used as adverbs, meaning "so to speak" or "if that is the right word for it"
or "vaguely," as in *I sort of felt faint* and *I kind of imagined that
you might come*; these usages are also combated by the schools,
as being unnecessary and imprecise, but are very common in
speech; they are also undergoing the kind of phonetic change we
have already seen in *ought to*, and becoming ˈsɔːtə and ˈkaində.

It is becoming increasingly common to omit the relative
that, for example to say *a man I know* rather than *a man that I
know*. This is not new, but the balance of forms is shifting,
especially in speech, where *that* is becoming positively rare.
People are also beginning to omit the *that* from the phrase *now
that* and *so that*; the latter is still substandard, perhaps, but is
spreading, especially among the young; I recently saw an
example in one of the reputable political weeklies, where it was
said that *every adolescent yearns for a motor-bike, so he can see the
world*. On the other hand, *that* is now often used as an adverb
of degree (adjective-modifier) meaning "very," as in *it's not
that good* (used absolutely). The word *very* is now frequently
used in places where people would formerly have said *much* or
very much; one such place is before a past participle (*very
interested, surprised, upset*), which means in effect that such
participles are becoming adjectives (as others have before them,

e.g., tired); another place is before certain adverbs like *astray* and *wrong*; I recently heard a distinguished musician speaking on the B.B.C. say *I can't go very wrong if.* . . .

It is also possible that changes are taking place in the use of the definite article: it is very often omitted in positions where it would formerly have been normal. The newspapers and the B.B.C., for example, talk about *the necessity for raising Bank Rate*, where one might have expected *the Bank Rate*; people often say *in U.S.A.*, instead of *in the U.S.A.*; and the B.B.C. now calls one of its publications *Radio Times*, whereas it used to say *The Radio Times*. Other words with which I have noticed this are *government*, *university*, *temperature*, *State Department*, and words like *theatre* and *cinema*; a well-known English dramatist recently wrote "The face of this country now emerges . . . most vigorously from television, cinema, and theatre"; and a B.B.C. news-bulletin announced "General de Gaulle is to speak to the nation on radio and on television" (compare the more old-fashioned phrase *on the wireless*). It is difficult to say whether such changes are going to have any long-term significance.

Some changes of usage are also arising by the *contamination* of one construction by another. A simple example is the confusion (common in Present-day English) between *from A to B* and *between A and B*; this has led to the new construction *between A to B*; for example, the B.B.C. weather-forecasters often tell us that *the temperature will be between 35 to 40 degrees*. Similar is the confusion between the type *not more than 50* and the type *from 40 to 50*; this gives a mixed construction *not more than 40 to 50* (which hardly means anything more than *not more than 50*): but this may be an example of confused logic rather than of contaminated syntax. Another contamination that is now very common is between the verbs *consist of* and *comprise*, producing the form (now common in reputable publications) *comprise of*; there is a similar contamination of *comprise* by *be composed of*, giving the form *be comprised of*. There has probably also been confusion between *there is no question of* "there is no likelihood (or intention) of" and *there is no question but that* "there is no doubt that"; this, at any rate, seems a likely explanation of the ambiguity of the expression *there is no question that*, which some people use to mean "there is no doubt that," while others (a minority) use it to mean "there is no likelihood (intention) that."

A very characteristic development of Modern English is the great growth of compound verbs or verb-phrases, especially ones consisting of verb plus adverb. The verb-adverb combination must be distinguished from the verb followed by a preposition-phrase. The difference can be seen in *he ran down the road* and *he ran down his rival*; in the first, *ran* is a simple verb, and *down* goes with *the road*; in the second, *ran down* is a compound verb (meaning "depreciate, disparage"), and *his rival* is its object. There are prosodic differences between the two sentences: in the first there is a slight pause between *ran* and *down*, whereas in the second the pause is between *down* and *his*; and normally the word *down* would be stressed in the second sentence but not in the first. The two sentences also behave differently syntactically; the first can be twisted round to give *the road down which he ran*, but from the second we cannot form *the rival down whom he ran*; and if we replace *road* and *rival* by pronouns, the first becomes *he ran down it* and the second *he ran him down*, with a characteristic difference of word-order.

In the whole of the Modern English period there has been a great proliferation of these compound verbs (another sign of the analytic tendencies in the language); a glance at any good dictionary will show what an enormous number there are: for example, look up the verbs *get*, *put*, and *try*. Moreover, new combinations are being formed still, and new meanings given to existing ones. Recent examples of transitive compound-verbs are *shrug off*, "treat with indifference"; *build up*, "advertise" (new meaning); *start up*, "set (an engine) in motion"; *fall for*, "be captivated by, taken in by"; and *brew up*, "brew." *Brew up* can also be intransitive, in the sense "develop, be in process of formation" (*there's a storm brewing up*); another verb that can be either transitive or intransitive is *bomb up*, "load with bombs"; here the *up* has the force of "completely," as often in compound verbs (*eat up*, *burn up*). Examples of recent intransitive compound verbs are *ice-up*, "become coated with ice"; *lose out*, "lose"; *butt in*, "interfere, intervene"; and the two colloquial phrases meaning "depart", *push off* and *push along*.

Often, a compound verb is followed by a preposition, and

sometimes the combination has a special meaning of its own; recent examples are *walk out on*, "desert, abandon"; *gang up on* or *gang up against*, "combine against"; *face up to*, "confront, not shrink from"; *fix up with*, "supply with"; *get away with*, "do with impunity"; and *meet up with*, "meet." Such popular compounds can often be paraphrased by a single learned word (*walk out on—abandon*); in other cases the particles tacked on after the verb are mere linguistic exuberance: in Britain, *meet up with* means no more than *meet* (though in America it has existed for over a century in the sense "overtake" or "fall in with").

Another analytic construction which seems to be spreading is the phrase consisting of verb plus object, instead of a simple verb. Thus we often say *to have a look at* instead of *to look at*, and *give me a ring* instead of *ring me* ("telephone me").

For several changes, I have mentioned American influence as an accelerator; in most cases, I think, it is just this; it encourages developments that are already taking place in Britain anyway. There are some changes, however, which are probably due entirely to American influence, and I have picked on two examples of incipient change in British English which are probably of this kind. The first is a point of word-order. There is a group of adverbs (many of them adverbs of frequency or indefinite time) which can be used immediately before the verb: *I always walk to the office*; *he never drinks beer*; *you scarcely know him*; and so on. If, however, the verb contains an auxiliary, then in British English the adverb is placed between the auxiliary and the base-form of the verb: *I can always walk to the office*; *he is always drinking*; *you would scarcely know*; and so on. The adverb is only placed *before* the auxiliary if the auxiliary is to be given special emphasis: *I always* CAN *walk to the office*; *he often* IS *seen there*; and so on. In American English, however, the adverb is often put before the auxiliary without implying any special stress on the auxiliary: American *he often is seen there* beside British *he's often seen there*. This American usage is now sometimes seen and heard in Britain, especially in journalism. The second example has to do with the negative and interrogative forms of the verb *to have*. When *have* is a full verb (meaning *possess, hold, experience*, etc.), not an auxiliary, it has two ways of forming its negative and interrogative: (1) with parts of the auxiliary *do* (*do you have?*, *he didn't have*, etc.); and (2) without using *do* (*have you?*, *he hadn't*, or in British usage very often *have you got?*, *he hadn't got*). The distribution of these two types in British English is rather complicated, and depends partly on the meaning of *have*: thus we say *he hadn't got any money*, but *he didn't have any difficulty*. In some cases, however, it also depends whether or not the verb denotes *habitual* action: thus we say *Do you have dances in your village hall?* (habitual), but *Have you got a dance on to-night?* (not habitual). This habitual/non-habitual criterion is not typical of American usage, which often employs *do*-forms for non-habitual *have*, where British English employs *got*-forms: thus Americans often say *Do you have the time?*, where Englishmen say *Have you got the time?*. Here again, American English is now beginning to influence British English, and usages of the type *Do you have the time?* are creeping (though slowly) into fashion.

Finally, I should like to call attention to a few changes which are perhaps as much stylistic as syntactic. The first can be classed as a syntactic development which gives a distinctive stylistic effect: this is the tendency for almost any noun to be used in close apposition with a person's name, as if it were a title. Formerly, there were only a few nouns that could be used in this way: we could talk of *Professor Smith*, *Captain Brown*, *Mr Jones*, *the River Thames*, and so on: but it was a select list. Recently the habit has grown of using any noun denoting a rank, profession, or occupation in this way: so that people talk about *Prime Minister Macmillan*, where formerly they would have said either *the Prime Minister*, *Mr Macmillan*, or *Mr Macmillan*, *the Prime Minister*. Recent examples which I have heard in B.B.C. news-bulletins are *centre-forward John Smith*, *actress Flora Robson* and *trainer Vincent O'Brien*; but any day's listening or newspaper-reading will produce a large crop. Moreover, the habit has grown up of adding modifiers to the noun, so that we hear of *Army Captain Brown* and *Cambridge Professor Smith*; formerly, it would have been necessary to say either *Professor Smith of Cambridge*, or *the Cambridge professor*, *Smith*. Lately, other kinds of nouns have come to be used in this way, so that we read about *Birmingham housewife Mrs Smith* (*instead of Mrs Smith, a Birmingham housewife*) and *teenager Mary*

Smith (instead of *Mary Smith, a teenager*). This began, in England at any rate, as a newspaper usage, probably under American influence: but now it is also very common on the wireless, and is beginning to be heard in ordinary speech.

The second change is on the borderline between syntax and style. It is the growing habit (especially in newspapers and on the wireless) of inserting parenthetic sentences. Most often these parentheses could easily have been adjective clauses: a typical example is *Boxer Bill Smith* (*he will be twenty-four to-morrow*) *has signed a contract to fight* . . .; here the *he* could easily be replaced by *who*; and in effect we here have a tendency to replace subordinate clauses by a paratactic construction. Sometimes, however, the parenthesis is not obviously a replacement for a clause in this way; here are two examples heard on the B.B.C. news: *Her atomic bomb* (*there's been no official statement yet about its size*) *was detonated* . . .; and *With Mr Khruschev in Delhi* (*it's the second day of his visit*), *Mr Nehru said* . . . . Anybody can collect scores of examples simply by listening to the wireless or reading the newspapers for a few hours. The object of these parentheses, it seems, is to make the style less formal, more colloquial; perhaps it is felt that a formal clause-structure with main-subordinate relations is more than ordinary people can take; if so, this may be significant for the future of English. In the meantime, it is merely an irritating mannerism of the mass-media.

The third point is purely stylistic, and concerns sentence-length. There is some evidence to show that, in written English (at least in novels), sentences have got shorter during the past fifty years; at the same time, there has been a decline in the number of continuative relative-clauses (*i.e.,* non-defining or non-restrictive ones). It is difficult to say whether this bears any relation to changes in *speech*-habits, but it may do; the evidence of literature suggests that our ancestors (at least the educated ones) spoke in a more deliberate and measured way than we do. We must treat literary evidence with caution, since we know that plays and novels are not slices of life: but we cannot disregard it. We do know, for example, that until relatively recent times an educated Englishman regarded conversation as an art, as something to be trained in and practised; and we know that the Renaissance gentleman prized the study of rhetoric for practical purposes, as part of his political training. It does look as though, on the whole, our speech is tending to greater fragmentation, to looseness of structure; we avoid formally constructed periods, we change constructions in the middle, we leave sentences uncompleted. If you can get hold of a tape-recorder, try leaving it running for an hour while your family or friends carry on an ordinary conversation in ignorance of it; when you play it back, you will be shocked at the disconnected, fragmentary, shapeless quality of the language used. We may well be on the eve of a change in which the large-scale formal structures of the language, now largely preserved in writing, will be broken down and replaced by smaller syntactic units loosely connected.

Chapter VI:

Notes and suggestions for further reading

On English grammar generally, see the various diachronic and synchronic grammars referred to at the end of Chapter I. On syntax, see also C. T. Onions, *An Advanced English Syntax* (London 1904), and Eugen Einenkel, *Geschichte der Englischen Sprache: II Historische Syntax* (Strassburg, 3rd edn., 1916). On morphology, see E. A. Nida, *Morphology: the Descriptive Analysis of Words* (2nd edn., Ann Arbor 1949). An important book for the advanced student is Noam Chomsky, *Syntactic Structures* ('s-Gravenhage 1957), which discusses the basic theory of grammatical analysis. For the grammar of Present-day English, see especially Barbara M. H. Strang, *Modern English Structure* (London 1962). A good up-to-date work on English usage is A. S. Hornby, *A Guide to Patterns and Usage* (Oxford 1954); also useful is Palmer and Blandford, *A Grammar of Spoken English* (Cambridge 1939); these two books are designed for foreign learners of English, but are also useful for the native student.

On the grammar of modern American English, see (in addition to the works mentioned at the end of Chapter I) C. C. Fries, *The Structure of English* (New York 1952, London 1957), and H. Whitehall, *Structural Essentials of English* (New York 1951, London 1958).

As examples of detailed monographs within the field of historical English syntax, see Alvar Ellegård, *The Auxiliary Do* (Stockholm 1953), and Göran Karlberg, *The English Interrogative Pronouns* (Stockholm 1954). As an example of a detailed monograph in the field of Present-day English syntax, see Frank Behre, *Meditative-Polemic Should in Modern English That-Clauses* (Stockholm 1955).

The work of Mossé's referred to is the one already mentioned at the end of Chapter I.

Chapter VII

Epilogue

THIS book will have been useful if it has sharpened your awareness of what is going on around you. If you are an amateur, you will probably not ask for more. If, however, you hope to become a professional, then your further progress will depend on the active work that you yourself undertake. For example, if you want to study historical English linguistics, then you must undertake detailed work on actual texts: books on the history of the English language will never get you beyond the surface: to get below it, you must yourself read and study the language as it existed in previous ages. If you want to get anywhere in synchronic linguistics, then you must undertake pieces of actual analysis of part of a language.

If this book has given you a greater interest in the living language, why not try doing a little analysis on your own account? Begin with your own speech, thus limiting the field and making sure that your informant is available whenever you want him. Try, for example, to give systematic accounts of the following in your own speech.

1 *The way nouns form their plurals*

As you are dealing with speech, not writing, your description must be in phonetic terms, not in terms of spelling. For example, the nouns *cat* and *dog*, in terms of spelling, both form their plural by adding an -*s*, but the -*s* represents different sounds in the two cases. You may find that you can cover most cases by fairly simple rules, but that there are a number of nouns that do not conform to the rules; if you cannot see any way of fitting these nouns into your system, you will simply have to give them as a list of exceptions.

2 *The way verbs form their past simple tense* (walk/walked, run/ran, etc.)

Here you will find the "exceptions" even more troublesome, but you may be able to organise them into partial systems. As with the plurals of nouns, describe your usage in phonetic terms, not in terms of spelling.

3 *The order in which the modifiers of a noun occur*

For example, in the phrase *an old grey stone wall, covered with moss*, we have the headword *wall* and as noun-modifiers the adjectives *old* and *grey*, the noun *stone*, and the adjective phrase *covered with moss*; in your own speech, could these have occurred in a different order? Can you draw up a set of rules that describe your usage in general in this matter? You will probably find it necessary to divide up noun-modifiers into a number of different classes.

4 *The order in which adverbs and adverb phrases occur in a sentence*

Can you give a systematic account of adverb-order in your own speech? As with adjectives, you will probably find it necessary to classify adverbs and adverb-phrases into different types. (Do not take into account the so-called "adverbs of degree," like *very*: these have a different function, and are a separate problem.)

5 *The use of* "some" *and* "any"

Do you say, for example, *Will you have some more tea?* or *Will you have any more tea??* Have these two sentences got different meanings in your own speech, that is, would you use them in different situations? If so, can you define the difference? Try to give a general account of the use of *some* and *any* in your own speech, and also of *somebody* and *anybody, something* and *anything*.

6 *The* "of"-*genitive and the* "'s-"*genitive*

Try to discover what your own usage is. You will probably find it helpful to classify nouns into different groups, on the lines hinted at in Chapter 6: but you may also have to take into account the construction in which the genitive occurs; for example, do you tend to avoid a construction like *the A of the B of the C*, and to say instead *the A of the C's B*?

7 *The expression of future time*

How many different ways have you of expressing futurity? Two different ways are seen, for example, in *I go to London to-morrow*, where we have a present-simple tense and an adverb of time, and *I shall go to London*, where we have a future-simple tense. Can you give an account of the various situations in which you use these different forms?

8 *The contrast between present-simple and present-continuous tenses*

When do you use the present simple (*I walk*), and when the present-continuous (*I am walking*)? Try to give a systematic account of the different situations in which you use each. Remember that the situation may be different for different kinds of verbs: do not assume that what is true for *walk* will necessarily be true for *see*, for *have*, or for *be*.

One could suggest many more such exercises, but I have given you enough to keep you busy for quite a time. The first two exercises are fairly straightforward, but the other six are complicated. I cannot give you any set of "right answers" to them. For one thing, you are trying to analyse your own usage, and only you know what that is. Of course, grammarians have attempted to give answers to them for "standard English" in general, and you will find fairly full accounts of them in a number of the grammars listed at the end of Chapters I and VI: but do not assume that the last word has been said on any of these questions by any grammarian. Anybody who has taught English as a foreign language knows that, however complicated the rules may be in any given grammar-book, it is nearly always possible to controvert them by finding an example that does not fit. One reason for this, of course, is that there are quite considerable differences between different groups of the community (even within "educated" groups), and even between individuals within a group. And then there is the fact of linguistic change, which must make any grammar-book out-of-date on some points within a period of twenty years or so. So altogether it is best to maintain an attitude of healthy (though respectful) scepticism towards the grammars, and to be quite prepared to make a different analysis of your own. But don't claim too much for your analysis, even if it seems watertight: it will be a description of your own usage, or perhaps of the usage of a small group around you: do not rashly assume that it will necessarily hold for other groups within the language-community.

If you are not a native speaker of English, you cannot of course embark on such analyses of your own spoken English (or rather, it would not be profitable for you to do so). I suggest, however, that it would be profitable for you to carry out similar analyses on your speech in your native tongue. Indeed, your own speech in the mother-tongue, and the speech of the people around you, is always the right place to begin language-study. Once again, try to approach your own language with a fresh eye, uncorrupted by the grammar you were taught at school; for, unless your country is more fortunate than most, the grammar you were taught at school probably included a good deal of nonsense.

Whether you are a native speaker of English or not, the scientific study of the language, both historical and descriptive, has much to offer: both as a discipline in its own right, and as an ancillary instrument in other studies (literature, history, anthropology, sociology), it has its contribution to make to that understanding, and consequent control, of our environment (both human and non-human) which is the end of learning. I hope that this book may have made a small contribution to this end, if only by pointing to some of the things which are going on around all of us, and thereby making us more conscious of them; by making us more conscious of the social forces operating around and in us, and of the pervasive part played by language in all their operations.

Index

In cases where a concept or technical term is explained or defined, and then used throughout the book, a reference is given only for the original explanation or definition

adjectives, comparison of: 131-2.
adverbs: 137-9, 140-1, 147.
affixes: 80-83.
affricates: 52.
Afrikaans: 100.
Alfred the Great: 4-5, 8, 15.
allomorph: 87.
allophone: 36.
American-English: 44, 49, 51, 75.
American influence: 20-22, 101-2, 141-3.
American Speech: 14.
Amis, Kingsley: 27.
analogy: 59-60.
angry young men: 26-7.
appositions: 142-3.
Armstrong, L. E.: 75.
Arnold, Thomas: 22.
articles: 6, 139.
assimilation: 62-4.
Australian-English: 46, 49.
auxiliaries: 3, 134-7, 141-2.
auxiliary verbs: *see* auxiliaries.

back-formation: 70, 94.
Barber, C. L.: 13, 127.
Baugh, A. C.: 13.
Behre, Frank: 145.
Berg, P. C.: 106-7.
Bergman, G.: 107.
Björkman, E.: 106.
Blandford, F. G.: 144.
blends: 89.
Bloch, B.: 75.
Boethius: 14.
Bradley, H.: 13.
Braine, John: 27.
Bréal, Michel: 127.
Brook, G. L.: 13, 31.

calques: 100-1.
cardinal vowels: 39-40.
Carroll, Lewis: 89.
Cassidy, F. G.: 13.
Chaucer, G.: 1, 3-4, 5, 7, 8, 15.
Chomsky, N.: 144.
Cohen, A.: 75.
combinative changes: 42.
comparison of adjectives: 131-2.
complementary distribution: 36.
compound verbs: 140-1.
compound words: 83-8.
Congreve, W.: 23.
conjunctions: 137-8.
consonants: 51-3; devoicing of: 56-7; intrusive: 57-60; loss of 53-6; voicing of: 57.
contamination: 139-40.
"Continental" pronunciations: 72-4.
conversion: 91-4.
Curme, G. O.: 13.

Danish: 134.
definite article: 139.
De Saussure, F.: 10, 12.
devoicing of consonants: 56-7.
diachronic linguistics: 10-11.
dialect-mixing: 18-21, 64.
Dialect Survey of England: 19, 31.
dialects, regional: 11, 16-17, 18-19; and social: 17-18.
Diesel, Rudolf: 95.
Dieth, Eugen: 31.
diphthongs: 40-41.
Dobson, E. J.: 76.

educational system: 18-20, 22-3, 25-6, 73.

Einenkel, E.: 144.
Ekwall, E.: 76.
Eliot, T. S.: 1.
Elizabeth I: 2, 3, 4, 14-15.
Ellegård, Alvar: 15, 144.
Empson, W.: 127-8.
English Language Teaching: 14.
English Studies: 14.
equivocation: 109-10.
euphemism: 124-6.
extension of meaning: 115-17.

Fielding, Henry: 23.
figurative language: 122-3.
Firth, J. R.: 13.
Fowler, H. W.: 9.
Francis, W. N.: 14, 75.
French: 5, 72-3, 78, 98-9.
fricatives: 52.
Fries, C. C.: 144.
function words: 7.

German: 5, 72, 99-100, 133.
Gilliéron, Jules: 32.
Gimson, A. C.: 74-5.
Gleason, H. A.: 13.
glottal stop: 60-1.
grammar: 129.
grammatical change: 129-45.
Greek: 55, 78-80, 98.

Hill, A. A.: 14, 75.
Hockett, C. F.: 13.
homophony: 104-5.
Hornby, A. S.: 144.
hybrids: 83.

Icelandic: 1.
inflexions: 2, 4, 5-6, 129-32.
initials: 97-8.
intensity, loss of: 123-4.
internal loans: 101-3.
intrusive consonants: 57-60.
inverse spelling: 136.
isolative changes: 41.
Italian: 55, 72.

Jespersen, O.: 13, 76.
Jones, Daniel: 23-4, 31, 35, 39-42, 44-5, 50, 63, 64, 74, 75, 86.

Karlberg, G.: 144.
Kingdon, R.: 75.
Kruisinga, E. A.: 13.
Kurath, H.: 13.

Lancaster, Osbert: 89, 107.
lateral consonant: 52.
Latin: 5, 73-4, 78-80, 98, 130, 133.
Leisi, Ernst: 14.
length of vowels: 38, 49-50; changes in: 50-1.
linguistic change, pace of: 1, 8; types of: 6.
lip-rounding: 40.
loan-translations: 100-1.
loan-words: 5, 98-101.
loans, internal: 101-3.
loss of consonants: 53-6.
loss of intensity: 123-4.
loss of words: 104-6.
Luick, Karl: 13.

MacCarthy, P. A. D.: 74.
McIntosh, A.: 31.
malapropisms: 111-12.
marked forms: 105-6, 107.
mass media: 19-20.
meaning, changes in: 6, 108-28.
metaphor: 122-3.
Middle English: 8.
Mitford, Nancy: 29, 31.
Modern English: 8.
modifiers of nouns: 147.
morpheme: 84-5.
morphology: 6-7, 129.
Mossé, F.: 14, 135, 145.
Motor: 100.
Murdoch, Iris: 132.

narrowing of meaning: 115, 117-20.
nasal consonants: 52.
nasalisation: 40.

N.E.D.: see *New English Dictionary*.
New English: 8.
New English Dictionary: 77, 78, 106.
newspaper headlines: 104, 126-7.
Nida, E. A.: 107, 144.
Nielsen, Harald: 100.
nonce-word: 77.
noun modifiers: 147.
noun plurals: 146.

of-genitive: 132-3, 147-8.
Ogden, C. K.: 127.
Old English: 4, 5, 8, 37, 54-5.
Onions, C. T.: 144.
opaque words: 80, 111-12.
Orton, H.: 31.
Osborne, John: 26.
Oxford English Dictionary: 106.

Palmer, H. E.: 144.
Palmer, L. R.: 13.
parentheses: 143.
Partridge, E. H.: 107.
permutation: 109-10.
phoneme: 35-6.
phonetic symbols: 33-5, 75-6.
Pickles, Wilfred: 20.
Pike, K. L.: 75.
place-names: 69-70, 76.
plosives: 52.
plural of nouns: 146.
polysemy: 108-9.
Pope, Alexander: 1.
Potter, Simeon: 12, 13.
Poutsma, H. A.: 13.
prefixes: 81-2.
prepositions: 137-8, 140-1.
prescriptionists: 8-9.
Priestley, J. B.,: 17, 32.
pronunciation-changes: 7-8, 33-76;
    types of: 36-7.
proper names: 95-6.
prosodic changes: 37, 65-6.
public schools: 22-4, 25.
Puttenham, G.: 23, 31.

quality of vowels: 39-40; changes in:
    41-9.
Quirk, Randolph: 14, 107.

Raleigh, Sir Walter: 23, 31.
Reaney, P. H.: 76.
Received Pronunciation: 22-5.
Received Standard: 18, 20, 22-31.
Regional Standard: 27-8.
relative, omission of: 138.
resonants: 52.
revivals: 95.
Richards, I. A.: 127.
Ridpath, Philip: 14.
Roberts, Paul: 13.
Robertson, Stuart: 13.
Ross, Alan: 29-31.
R.P.: *see* Received Pronunciation.
R.S.: *see* Received Standard.
Rudskoger, A.: 127.
Russian: 28, 100.

Sapir, Edward: 13.
Savory, T. H.: 107.
Scandinavian: 98.
Schubiger, M.: 75.
scientific words: 78-80, 98.
semantic change: 6, 108-28.
semi-vowels: 52-3.
sentence-length: 143-4.
Serjeantson, M. S.: 106.
Shakespeare, W.: 1, 3, 37, 111.
Shaw, G. B.: 16.
Sheard, J. A.: 106.
Sheridan, R. B.: 111.
shortening: 89-91.
Skeat, W. W.: 31.
slang: 102-3.
Smith, A.: 107.
sonorants: 52.
specialisation of meaning: 115, 117-20.
spelling: 7; inverse: 136.
spelling pronunciations: 66-71.
Standard English: *see* Received Stan-
    dard.
Stern, Gustaf: 109-10, 127.
stops: 52.
Strang, Barbara M. H.: 13, 144.
stress, changes of: 65-6.
Stubelius, S.: 127.
Sturtevant, E. H.: 13.
subjunctive: 4, 5, 133-4.
suffixes: 82.
superlative of adjectives: 131-2.
Swedish: 55, 71, 100, 134.

syllable: 40-41.
synchronic linguistics: 10-11.
syntax: 7, 129.
system in language: 10.

tenses of verbs: 147, 148.
titles: 142-3.
trade names: 95-6.
Trager, G. L.: 75.
transcriptions, phonemic and allophonic: 33-6, 75-6.

U and non-U: 29-31.
Ullmann, S.: 108, 127.
unmarked forms: 105-6, 107.

verb phrases: 140-1.
verb tenses: 147, 148.
verbs, auxiliary: *see* auxiliaries.
vocabulary: 6, 77-107.
voice: 53.
voicing of consonants: 57.

vowel-diagram: 39.
vowel length: 38, 49-50; changes in: 50-1.
vowel quality: 39-40; changes in: 41-9.
vowels: 38-41.

Ward, Ida C.: 41, 42, 74, 75.
weak forms: 64.
Weekley, E.: 106.
West, Mae: 95.
Whitehall, H.: 144.
widening of meaning: 115-17.
Wilson, Harold: 125.
word-formation, methods of: 78-98.
word order: 5, 130, 141-2, 147.
words: 83-6; loss of: 104-6; opaque: 80, 111-12; scientific: 78-80, 98.
Wrenn, C. L.: 13.
Wright, E. M.: 13, 76.
Wright, J.: 13, 31, 76, 107.
Wyld, H. C.: 13, 31, 72.

Zandvoort, R. W.: 13, 106-7.